"Cecil F. Alexander wrote the words to .... Let Me Go.' The very first stanza says: 'O Love that will not let me go, / I rest my weary soul in Thee; / I give Thee back the life I owe, / That in Thine ocean depth its flow may richer, fuller be.'

"*The Lover of My Soul* is a heart-moving book detailing in honest and vulnerable ways the emptiness of a life apart from Christ. But what glues one's attention to the book is not only how the love of God drew Hanan to the Savior, but the suffering encountered even after the emptiness of her life had been filled with Christ. Time and time again when it would have seemed best just to throw up her hands and say, 'No more. I quit,' she finds herself continually drawn by those divine cords of love to the very Lover of her soul. The Lover of her soul becomes the satisfier of her soul.

"*The Lover of My Soul* is a book about learning to rest one's weary soul in God. It is a moving story of one giving her life back to God because of all His wonderful acts of love toward her. One cannot help but feel in reading the book that here is a woman who has discovered what it means to swim in the ocean depths of His infinite love. Here she has found not just security, but satisfaction! She has tasted the love of God.

"I heartily endorse this book for anyone to read. Oftentimes, the clouds of affliction block our view of the Lover of our soul. This book will remind you that no matter how thick those clouds His love is there. And if you are one who thinks that God's love and suffering are incompatible, then this book will show you how those cords of love are intended to draw you to Him. He wants you to find the satisfaction, like Hanan, of swimming in the ocean depths of His love. There you will find Him to be the Lover of your soul."

—*Don Winter, Senior Pastor*
Evangelical Community Church
Jackson, Tennessee

"Suffering is the path to holiness. Suffering is required on our journey toward becoming more Christlike. This is a beautiful story of how the trials and tribulations of life drew my mother from paganism to the loving arms of Christ."

—*Omar Hamada, M.D.*
Memphis, Tennessee

"I am truly blessed to have such a godly mother, who truly loves God with all her heart, soul, and mind. Her strength and fortitude amaze me as I think of all the struggles and difficulties she has been through. In spite of it all, her faith has remained true and her trust in God unshaken. She has experienced the intensity of God's love, and thus has been able to deeply love others with a sincere heart."

—*Sandy (Hamada) Combs, M.A.*

Lover
OF MY
SOUL

Lover
OF MY
SOUL

HANAN HAMADA

WINEPRESS WP PUBLISHING

Packaged by WinePress Publishing, PO Box 1406, Mukilteo, WA 98275. The views expressed or implied in this work do not necessarily reflect those of WinePress Publishing. Ultimate design, content, and editorial accuracy of this work is the responsibility of the author.

Names of some extended family and friends have been changed to protect their privacy.

All quotations are from the New King James Version of the Bible.

ISBN 1-57921-122-4
Library of Congress Catalog Card Number: 98-60752

For your Maker is your husband,
The LORD of hosts is His name;
And your Redeemer is the Holy One. . . ;
He is called the God of the whole earth.

ISAIAH 54:5

THE LOVER OF MY SOUL

An extraordinary love story of an Arab Druze and her God. . . .

A Lebanese immigrant bride who came to the United States at age seventeen and her dynamic story of struggle and searching to satisfy her thirsty soul. . . .

The hardships, barriers, suffering, and loneliness of life without God and the end of her search in the discovery of the true meaning of satisfaction, peace, joy, and victory in and through Jesus Christ the Lord. . . .

Dedication

This book was born as a result of my dear father's physical death. He left to be with my heavenly father. I dedicate it to:

- My wonderful, tender, loving mother
- My caring and sacrificial brothers; my only beloved sister
- Also to my dear husband, Louis Bahjat, whom God used as the main instrument to bring me to Himself and to make me in His image
- My precious children, Omar and Sandy, who God gave to us for blessing, comfort, and joy—two wonderful gifts to cherish for Him
- My God's chosen son and daughter-in-law (in-love), Andrew and Tara
- The precious firstborn grandchild, Nathan, who God gave us as a sweet reward, and the quiverful to come
- My beautiful Christian friends across the world, who helped me carry the load and the bitterness of the cross on my own thorny and rocky Golgotha path

And above all, to my Lord who is always there, where under His wings I will hide, in His arms I will fall, and whose feet I will wash with bitter tears of repentance, grief, and joy.

Acknowledgement

There is a friendship that God initiates and deepens in Him through the years. That is how it is with Elizabeth and me. This book was birthed in 1983 as a result of my father's death. God waited for my fifty-first birthday to bring about life to this book. Thank you, Elizabeth, for being His instrument and that in His appointed time you gave such a generous gift toward the publishing of this work. To God be the glory!

To Virginia Tait, for helping me with typing and editing; to Joy Morgan, for proofreading and retyping some of the manuscript. May we all enjoy the harvest together!

Contents

Introduction

It was October 10, 1982. The morning was bright and shimmering; the wind, cool and crisp. Trees burst with colors—some aflame, some sparkled like gold, some burnished like copper. From my kitchen window I admired the beauty of the southern United States.

What a great and wonderful God I have! Joyfully doing my chores, I praised and thanked God for His grace and mercy. I pondered Psalm 96:

> Oh, sing to the LORD a new song!
> Sing to the LORD, all the earth. . . .
> For the LORD is great and greatly to be praised. . . .
> Let the heavens rejoice, and let the earth be glad;
> Let the sea roar, and all its fullness;
> Let the field be joyful, and all that is in it.
> Then all the trees of the woods will
> rejoice before the LORD.

Night quickly descended. Omar and Sandy popped in from high school and departed for a youth party at the church. Loneliness and homesickness overshadowed me as I sat daydreaming in my parlor. The phone broke my reverie. My sister was calling from the Persian Gulf, some twelve thousand miles away.

"Hanan," she choked. "It's Dad."

"Dad!" I screamed, suddenly alert. "Did Dad? . . .

"No, Hanan, but—"

"But what, Maha?" I exclaimed.

"He survived a severe heart attack. His lung cancer is spreading seriously. Hanan, he asked about you. Come as soon as possible. But call first to make sure everything is OK."

A knot came to my throat. I swallowed hard and shivered. This news I had been dreading the ten years my beloved Lebanon had been in turmoil. The situation seemed to be ameliorating. But one never knows.

The next eighteen days passed like moments as I prepared to travel. Louis and I kissed our teenagers goodbye and headed in opposite directions. We cried and committed them to God. Driving to the Memphis airport, we claimed 1 Peter 5:7, "Casting all your care upon Him, for He cares for you."

Louis took me into his arms and sighed, "The Lord Himself will look after you. Remember what He said, 'I will never leave you nor forsake you.'" We parted to our planes, Louis flying west to California to lead a Bible conference; I, east to Lebanon.

After twenty-four tedious hours of travel, I heard the French captain announcing, "We're landing in Beirut this beautiful clear evening. It's seventy degrees."

My joy was unbounded! *Here I am at last!* When the doors opened, I rushed out to inhale my longed-for Lebanon! To my horror, the fragrance I had anticipated had been replaced by the smell of death. Tears fell from my eyes and a heavy feeling crushed my heart as I descended the ladder.

Collecting my luggage, the excitement of seeing my beloved family revived me. At the gate a multitude awaited the travelers. My eyes searched for a familiar face. Suddenly, I heard my brother call my name. As I turned to the sound of his voice, our eyes met. Exuberantly, we ran to each other and embraced.

"You've changed during these five and a half years, Walid," I cried.

"You, too," he replied, smiling.

The chauffeur stowed the luggage in the car and we were off. Darkness overshadowed Beirut. I smelled fire; the smoke was overpowering.

In my excitement I started talking loudly in mixed Arabic and English. Walid whispered, "Hanan, lower your voice, please. You could be heard outside. . . . It is good you reached us at night because the scenes would have been too shocking for you!"

We passed ruins and devastation. I stared into the darkness until we were stopped by soldiers at a checkpoint. One with a foreign accent asked for our papers. Walid rolled down his window and handed him the birth certificates and passports. He gazed inside and examined each of us before signaling us on. Another thirty minutes of ascending the mountain and we would reach my parents' home.

Mother, anxiously waiting, spied the car and hurried to greet me. "Hanan! Hanan! My daughter! I didn't believe I would live to see you again!" She showered me with hugs and kisses.

"Hanan," she said. "Your father is impatiently awaiting you. Run to him, my darling." I dropped my handbags and ran inside. Dad saw me and started weeping.

"Hanan!" He was struggling to get his words out. "My beloved, I am so glad to see you."

I bent down to him and took his beautiful snowy white head into my hands and together we wept. His wasted body shocked me. I tried to hide my feelings.

"Sit here so I can put my arms around you. Tell me, My life, are Omar and Sandy well? Tell me about them!"

Joyously, I reviewed the years that he had missed, the news for which he yearned. I fetched my purse and gave him their pictures. One by one he analyzed them; he kissed them; he cried.

"How they have grown!" he exclaimed. "I wish I could see them."

"Yes, Daddy," I responded. "You will see them someday."

The maid interrupted our conversation to serve tea and snacks.

Afterward, we helped him to his room and into bed, arranging pillows to ease his breathing. He kissed us all goodnight and quickly fell asleep.

Exhausted from the journey and excitement, I went to my room and spent most of the night agonizing before God, on my face in prayer. My heart was torn with grief. I wept to my dear Jesus. I could bear it no longer—the thought of losing my father. I asked God to prolong his life and give us a few good days together. His peace fell upon me and a verse of scripture came to me: "Come to Me, all you who labor and are heavy laden, and I will give you rest" (Matt. 11:28). Comforted, clinging to those words, I slept.

The sun shining into my room the next morning awakened me. Jumping out of bed and running down the stairs to check on Daddy, I found him already up, shaved, and showered.

"Daddy, how are you? You must be feeling better!"

"Yes," he reassured me.

"Daddy, can we go to the garden this morning?"

Placing two chairs in his rose garden, I hastily ran upstairs. Quickly, I dressed. I mustn't lose a moment. Joyfully, I thanked God for answering my prayer. Happiness boosted my energy. I praised the Lord for His great and mighty power! I wore my brightest dress and ran down to help Daddy brush his hair.

We strolled arm in arm as he showed me the beautiful fruit trees he had planted in my absence. He picked some fruit for me, watching my reaction with pleasure. We proceeded to his rose garden, admiring each creation. I cut a crimson rose and we sat down to talk.

"Daddy, please tell me about you and Mom." He smiled and thought for a while as he looked off toward the Mediterranean Sea, lost in reverie. He began to relate the most precious moments of his life. . . .

CHAPTER I

The Story of the Most Perfect Human Love I Know: Mom and Dad

A beautiful spring morning in 1930, a thirteen-year-old Lebanese girl stood between the roses in her garden balcony practicing her speech for drama class. Her name, Wafika, signifies tender, faithful, deep love. The sun was shining over the blue Mediterranean Sea. Through the air, the salty wind was blowing the scent of jasmine, henna, and roses.

Across the alley on top of a red brick-and-tile house, a handsome, energetic fifteen-year-old was supposed to be studying for his high school final examinations. He was distracted by the girl's piercing dark brown eyes. When their eyes met, he saw her cheeks turn red. Shyly, she tried to disappear between her roses.

Abraham Hussian's heart beat fast. *I adore her*, he mused. *I must finish high school early, and with grades high enough to enter medical school. I know that the mayor of Schweifat, Salah Ibrahim, would require the suitor for his only child to be successful. Besides, medicine is one of the highest callings a human could offer his God and humanity.*

His love grew day by day. His soul thirsted for her. How could he reveal his love in a culture that condemned adolescent love? One day, he borrowed her English literature book and wrote his name and hers in the drama of *Romeo and Juliet*.

She returned his love secretly in her heart, exclusively. Her ravishing brown eyes had reflected his image since early childhood.

News the next year that Wafika was leaving with her parents for South America devastated Abraham. He clung to the hope that she would return single to her ancestral estate which was being maintained by servants. Six years away from his beloved seemed like a century. His love for her grew daily.

Graduation from medical school in 1937 brought double joy. The Ibrahim's gardener and housekeeper revealed that their Wafika and her family would soon be resettling in Lebanon. Hope for marriage dominated his thoughts. The Druze culture expected the man not only to have a good profession, but also to have money for a superb wedding, jewelry, and trousseau. To this end, for three long years of practicing medicine, Abraham lived frugally.

In 1940 the great day arrived. In accordance with the Lebanese tradition, Abraham and his parents visited Mayor Salah Ibrahim. With her maid's help, Wafika selected her loveliest dress and jewels. She entered the formal living room, where special guests were welcomed.

At twenty-three, she was more glamorous than ever. In vain, numerous suitors had asked for her hand. The sight of Abraham set her eyes to sparkling and her heart to dancing. It was a dream come true! Elated, Abraham's eyes penetrated hers! This was the day both had eagerly awaited.

Mr. Hussian asked Mayor Ibrahim if he would accept Abraham as his son-in-law. The mayor, hating to part with his daughter, asked for time to consider and to consult with Wafika and her mother. Individually, the young couple prayed for a favorable reply. Reluctant to release his only child, he delayed one day, then another. Still he did not speak to Wafika or to her mother. Each day was like a month to the lovers. They lost their appetites for food and company. On the morning of the third day, Mayor Ibrahim approached the subject. He asked his wife, Daisy, if she had any objection. Wanting the best for her daughter and having confidence in Abraham, she agreed. Would Wafika accept the idea of Marriage to Abraham? Tears of joy flooded her eyes. Not wanting to sound too anxious, she modestly replied, "If you and mother think he is the best for me, I will try to be a good and faithful wife to him."

Abraham had not slept for three nights, anxiously awaiting the answer. On the same afternoon that Wafika's father gave his consent, there was a knock at the gate of the Hussian home. "Wafika's father, Mayor Ibrahim," announced the butler, "is requesting the honor of a visit from Abraham and his parents." Exuberantly, Abraham showered, shaved, and donned his best suit.

At eight o'clock that evening, they arrived and were greeted with the warm traditional Lebanese greetings of *"Ahlan wa Sahlan"* (welcome). Mrs. Ibrahim signaled for the fruit and pastries which Wafika served before sitting down.

The mayor addressed his honored guests, "We would like for the two families to unite in marriage, after an appropriate engagement period of adjustment for the bride and groom." Rose drinks were served as wedding plans were discussed. He explained the quality of jewelry and wardrobe he expected for his daughter. They dealt with the formal engagement and invitations and came to full agreement. Then the demitasse coffee was served, signaling the end of the visit.

The next morning Abraham visited his future bride. They sat on the balcony between the roses facing the blue Mediterranean Sea, enjoying each other's presence and talking about their plans. Time flew. Day after day their love flourished.

Abraham asked his prospective father-in-law to set a date for the formal engagement. Reluctantly, he agreed. The wedding rings were purchased. Relatives and friends were invited. The "Ajami," one of the best Lebanese restaurants, catered the food. Hors d'oeuvres and "Mezza," consisting of hundreds of famous Lebanese sweets. The tables were decorated with fresh fruit. Exotic Arabic and Lebanese music filled the background. The guests, caught up in the festivities, participated in the Lebanese folk dances. When the two families formally agreed on the engagement, the groom placed the wedding rings on his bride's right hand. Guests stayed until midnight, joyously celebrating the uniting of the two families.

The wedding was set for May 25, 1940. Abraham, Wafika, and her father daily patronized the "Souk," where Rome had left its imprint in bazaars and shops.

A tremendous variety of goods from every port were a vivid testimony to Lebanon's prosperity as a center of international exchange—where East and West met.

They ambled from shop to shop, buying the finest of fabrics and garments for Wafika's trousseau. They visited almost every gold shop along the mile-long street famous for handmade gold and diamond jewelry. They purchased whatever appealed to Wafika. Finally, they selected the wedding drinks, the sweets, and the hundreds of silver boxes filled with sugarcoated almonds for the wedding guests.

Two days before the wedding, Friday, May 23, the two families drove to the mountains of Baakline, Lebanon, accompanied by relatives. There they called upon the "Sheik-al-Akal," Sheik Hussian Hamada, leader of the religion. The marriage license was drawn up according to the law of the Druze, a unitarian religion and offshoot of the Shiite Muslims. After which the Sheik prayed over the couple, and a great celebration followed. Chocolate and coffee were served. Now they were legally married. What joy!

On Saturday the bride observed the cleansing processes demanded by the Druze culture. Sunday morning, makeup artists arrived to dress her hair and face and help her put on her lacy white and silver wedding gown and her exquisite veil.

Wafika mounted the flower bedecked platform in the big *Dar*. Sitting quietly on her "throne," she watched as more baskets of flowers arrived from guests. The fragrance was overwhelming. Guests filled the house and the balconies. They placed their gifts on decorated tables; they gazed on the bride; they chatted.

After a long hour, a messenger announced that the bridegroom was coming to take his bride. In he came with his family. The guests and families were seated. The groom removed the veil, kissed his bride, and took her away. The crowd followed to the groom's home where a great celebration lasted all afternoon. Abraham and Wafika departed for their honeymoon. The snow-covered mountain ranges contrasted with the waves of colors in the valleys, reminding the lovers of Persian tapestries. Colorful wildflowers filled the valleys. Blossom-laden fruit trees covered the mountain slopes. For a joy-filled week the newlyweds reveled in the beauty of God's creation.

Upon their return, an offer to attend Iraq's ruling family awaited them. Abraham accepted the invitation. That hop country contrasted with Lebanon's moderate climate and Wafika became ill. Worried about her health, her father immediately flew to Iraq. So unselfish was Abraham's love for her, that he allowed her father to escort Wafika back to Lebanon. Soon it became known that Wafika was expecting her first child. The name Marwan was given to the beautiful baby. In a month, Wafika, Marwan, and the mayor rejoined the new father. After Grandpa secured a nurse for the baby and a maid for Wafika, he returned to Lebanon.

Two years passed and Salah was born in their new location—Aley, a mountain resort in Lebanon. He was named after both grandfathers. Fair and handsome, Salah resembled his father.

Three years later Wafika was expecting her third child. How they wanted a girl! They believed God had given them the name, "Hanan," which means "tender, merciful, and compassionate love." Instead, Walid, the third son was born—fair and healthy. The cherub delightfully captivated their hearts.

Abraham and Wafika prayed and hoped that God would give them a girl. On March 10, 1947, Wafika was working in her flower bed enjoying the sunshine of the warm Mediterranean when she felt her first labor pains. She called her father. Without delay he, Aunt Latifa, and a neighbor-friend drove Wafika to the hospital in Beirut. There, a few hours later, I, Hanan, was born.

CHAPTER II

My Birth and Childhood

G od's answer to my parent's prayer had come! Grandfather Salah telegraphed his son-in-law who speedily flew to meet the daughter for whom he had been yearning. He loved me tenderly. I resembled my mother, which especially endeared me to him. Proudly, he carried me everywhere. One day I was in his lap as we were motoring to the mountains, and I regurgitated on his best suit. He patiently and lovingly cleaned himself and again carried me. A few months later he returned to Iraq but visited us often.

My maternal grandmother, Daisy, a bundle of love, lived with us after her divorce from the mayor (the first and only divorce in our family). She looked like an angel. This beautiful woman, with cheeks blushing like red apples, face beaming, eyes glittering with tenderness, and gleaming golden hair smelling as fresh as a daisy, talked to me as I contentedly cuddled in her lap. She initiated my awareness of God. Always smiling, her sweet and tender attitude was positive and encouraging.

After my two baby years in Aley, we moved back to our hometown, Schweifat—two blocks from my grandfather's home. It was lovely with fresh breezes from the Mediterranean Sea—warm and humid in the summer, generally moderate in winter.

Before I was three, Mother and her Aunt Latifa brought home a baby wrapped in a pink and white wool blanket with a dog printed on it. Was I excited to see my baby sister, Maha! How I loved our baby "doll"!

But all was not serene. Insecurity, vanity, and pride plagued me. To prove my superiority, when unsupervised I would sneak up to the nursery and pinch Maha hard enough to make her wake up and cry.

I doubt that I recognized the sin of vanity when the neighbor's older girls would come and play with my hair, combing it into a bun on top of my head and then heap on the compliments. Or the insecurity satisfied by my stuffed bear, Akram, that I loved and was my constant companion and "security blanket." When Father would come home frequently for several weeks, he would see my stubborn pride whenever he corrected me. I was good at throwing temper tantrums.

Another move, when I was five, took us to the country. Memories abounded from that home surrounded by terraces, grape vines, and fruit trees. Early mornings we raided the orchard. Wildflowers abounded in the rocks and fields: red and purple poppies, white and pink cyclamen, white and yellow daises, lilies, daffodils, and tulips. Maha and I spent hours picking bouquets for Mother, relatives, and friends. I was impressed with God in all the beauty of His creation, seeing His presence everywhere: "For since the creation of the world His invisible attributes are clearly seen, being understood by the things that are made, even His eternal power and Godhead; so that they are without excuse" (Rom. 1:20).

Maha and I played outside enjoying the moderate climate of Lebanon, excluded from the rough masculine games. One day my youngest brother Walid came running in agony. His elbow was turned inward as he fell playing soccer. Mother fainted—as was the norm when any of us got hurt. The maid threw orange-blossom water on her face to revive her. Later my two older brothers and mother walked two miles to the town's osteopath, a relative. He pushed the elbow into place. A Druze boy was expected to be manly and take pain, but it so overpowered him that he screamed and yelled anyway. Mother nearly repeated her act. Maha and I stayed home and prayed.

Another summer day, Maha and I were in our garden admiring the beauty of God's creation. A Lebanese is born a romantic and a lover of nature. Maha noticed a grapevine and we ran toward it. I bent over to see the luscious cluster of grapes. Maha wanted to see it, too. Bending over, she slipped and fell five feet down. Her head hit a broken glass. Blood gushed out and she screamed. Scared, I added my screams until mother and the maid came running to investigate. Seeing Maha, Mother's head started spinning. She cried to the maid to take the child. I followed fast on their heels, running to the house. Mother sent my brother to call the nearest relative, who initiated first aid. He ground coffee to powder and pushed it firmly on the wound to clot the blood. After the bleeding stopped and they cleaned the wound and bandaged her, mother turned to discipline me. I—not Maha's curiosity—was blamed for the whole ordeal.

I felt I had received an undue measure of the blame and sought refuge in God.

In 1950 my father relocated his medical practice to South America, where his two brothers were in business. Eager to provide well for us, he found the competition in small Lebanon too great. We felt lost without him. However, this separation was not unusual in Lebanon. It was commended as sacrifice for the financial stability of the family. Sadly, Maha did not remember my father. She used to ask Mother if Dad were young or old.

Mother was a tremendous homemaker, a good parent, a loving and faithful wife. Every penny my father sent, Mother used judiciously. She dressed the house and children tastefully and immaculately. In public, people gazed at us, admiring mother's ability. She also saved, collected, and invested in business. She surprised and pleased him with her wise investments of the small amounts he sent her. Father trusted her judgment totally.

That reminds me of the virtuous woman the Bible speaks about in the book of Proverbs, chapter 31.

> Who can find a virtuous wife?
> for her worth is far above rubies.
> The heart of her husband safely trusts her,
> so he will have no lack of gain.
> She does him good and not evil
> All the days of her life. . . .

It goes on to tell how she manages her business and home, and concludes with:

> Her children rise up, and call her blessed;
> Her husband also, and he praises her.

"Many daughters have done well, but you excel them
all."
Charm is deceitful, and beauty is vain:
But a woman who fears the LORD, she shall be praised.
Give her of the fruit of her hands;
And let her own works praise her in the gates.

Although we were naughty at times, mother seemed to
manage. Early one summer day she left us with Grandma
and the maid so she could search Beirut for an apartment
building to buy.

The previous day we had begged her—unsuccessfully—
to take us to the beach. After she left, the five of us went to
our big sunken Arabian bathroom and carefully closed all
the drainage holes. We filled the room with water and invited the neighbor kids for a swim.

Returning weary with her unsuccessful endeavors, she
was shocked at that sight. The water not only flooded the
bathroom, but also covered the marble floors in that part of
the house. Always patient, tender, and compassionate, she
corrected each one of us separately, less severely than we
had expected. She was a rock of refuge and a bundle of love
when we ran to her for comfort and security. What an awesome God to give me such a wonderful mother!

Every morning the maid swept the entire house, mopped
the floors, straightened up, and cooked the noon dinner.
Most people rested in the afternoon and then around four
o'clock went visiting. Mother never enjoyed visiting. Gos-
sip and small talk annoyed her—her time was precious.
But she was always pleasant, hospitable, and generous to
her visitors. She served fresh fruit, juices, and sweets and
terminated the visits with thick demitasse coffee.

Mother, however, always put us before the guests. After we came from school, we washed and had our dinner and fresh fruit. Mother then directed us in our studies. The maid frequently brought us some fruit or juice as a snack.

Mother, the maid, and sometimes Grandma all helped with our bathing before we retired. Bedtime stories of romance and adventures enthralled us; I used to wonder where our maid found them—*One Thousand and One Arabian Nights, Ali Baba, Sinbad, Cinderella, Snow White, Jane Eyre,* and others.

Late one night, Mother was packing to take us the next morning to the mountains. She heard footsteps; she saw the doorknob turning. Up she jumped, cried out to God, and with a fearful heart turned on the outside lights. "Who's there?" she yelled. She waited with a thumping heart. The intruder left and, in spite of her fears of his evil intentions, she slept.

The next morning we moved to the wonderful Druze town of Ainab, in the mountains, for the three summer months. The people were down-to-earth, hospitable, warm, and like one family.

Three local varieties of fig enhanced our breakfast. Other fruits—raspberries, grapes, and blueberries—satisfied every sweet tooth. Each morning the neighbors gathered for coffee and pizza. We children spent our time playing in the countryside, enjoying our friends and the delightful crisp weather.

Farmer Abou Rami appeared early one morning. Loudly and joyously, he called. My brothers and I responded to his invitation to accompany him to the harvest. He seated us on the yoke pulled by two bulls. Around the field we rode. I can still visualize that Lebanese farmer with his light brown, elongated felt cap wrapped with white cloth, his black baggy pants, white cotton shirt, and a colorful scarf around his waist. In spite of weather-worn skin, his features were mellow and his smile, tender.

At night the fun-loving, optimistic neighbors gathered for food, Lebanese music, and folk dancing. We had the time of our lives that summer. We would walk hand in hand every evening for miles—talking, visiting, singing, and enjoying the clean pine-and-cedar breeze.

Dad asked mother to join him in South America. She took Maha but enrolled my three brothers and me in the International Evangelical (boarding) School in Schweifat. The two eldest were in the boys' dorm. Walid (age eight, in fourth grade) and I (age six, in second grade) were in the girls'. My second cousin, Mona, a few years older than I, comforted, instructed, and mothered me. When I got scared at night, I would jump to her bed, next to mine.

Walid watched over me and protected me from some of the aggressive older girls. Occasionally, he treated me with a bar of candy, sacrificially purchased from his small allowance.

Our eldest brother Marwan was like my father. Six years my senior, he was the rock of my security. As leader and authority over the three of us, he was responsible for us. He had a tender heart and always thought of our well-being before his own.

Salah, the middle one, was also wonderfully unselfish. He carried out Marwan's orders and saw to it that Walid and I followed suit. Walid was a happy-go-lucky, chubby fellow and the terror of the school. When he got into trouble, Marwan would discipline him.

One night while Walid was still in the girls' dorm, he and his pal awoke at midnight. Carrying their mattresses, they walked up the hill to the boys' dorm, where they spent the rest of the night. In the morning the school principal had a severe punishment for him and so did Marwan.

I found it hard to live away from home and from the love and warmth of my family. Once when illness distressed me, I prayed to God. He came; He touched me; I woke up feeling fine, and I thanked Him for His loving care. One long weekend, many students went home. My cousin and I were homesick. Together we knelt and prayed, "Dear God, we love you. Please, God, you know that we are lonely. We miss our grandmothers. Please send them to us. Thank You." We opened our eyes; there were our grandmothers!

Great was our joy when we would receive permission from the school principal to spend a weekend in town with Grandmother. We dressed our best and alternately walked, skipped, ran, or ambled a few miles down the hill.

My favorite time to go was in the spring. The wind hit our faces, blew our hair, and seemed to carry us above the world. It whistled as it passed our ears and tickled our noses with the scents of the blossoms and flowers. As we walked among the grass and flowers of the field, we would stop to pick the yellow hemida plant to suck the tangy sap from its stem. We would pass Grandfather's orchards and sample his fruits—apricots, peaches, apples, tangerines, and green almonds. Leisurely, we picked tulips, poppies, and cyclamen for Grandma.

Through the old town's markets and antiquated streets we roamed, greeting friends and relatives who asked us about our parents. The medieval buildings with quadrilateral courtyards and gardens, the old Roman columns, and the gorgeous Arabian tunnels and arches fascinated me. We visited our relatives' homes, partook of their sweets, were warmly hugged and kissed and went on our way.

Our dear Grandma Daisy greeted us with joy and excitement. One by one, she held us close. Great Aunt Nuha who lived with her also expressed her affection. Together they asked about school, our grades, our activities, and our health.

From the time we entered until we left, Grandma kept bringing surprises. She was concerned that I was so thin and would coax, "Hanan, come here, Darling. Taste this for me please, Honey." Although I was disinterested in food, to please her I sampled all she prepared.

Her nineteenth-century mansion had a big wooden gate with iron bars swinging under curved Arabian arches. A few easy steps up led to the courtyard with gardens of jasmine, carnations, gardenias, and herbs, and a picturesque goldfish pool. To the left was her antiquated kitchen; across the courtyard, her Arabian bathroom; and facing the garden, her sitting room and her lovely bedroom with its huge, old, vaulted quadripartite arched ceiling.

A few steep rock steps and an ornate black-iron railing led to Aunt Nuha's slightly modernized four-room apartment. From her balconies we could view the sea, the airport, part of Beirut, some of the town of Schweifat, and the neighbors' houses.

After the *siesta*, peddlers would come with their tempting wares. They chanted funny words and songs. "Shortbread, shortbread, sweet, hot, and tasty. Taste it for only five piasters." "Ice cream, ice cream! Come on, you people. Come on down." "Oranges! Valley oranges, red and ripe." Auntie would lower her roped basket for the produce.

35

Grandma bought us the sweets—vanilla ice-cream balls covered with a chocolate shell; fruit-flavored popsicles; cotton candy (a pink kind); the delicious white candy made with Syrian goats' milk that looked like angel hair with pistachio nuts on top; and baked breads, cakes, and cookies. Even though I resisted the nutritious foods, I loved the treats. So unhappy was I at leaving Grandma and returning to school that my innards would rebel.

A year passed and news came of Mother's return to Lebanon and of Daddy going to New York for two years to specialize in pediatrics.

The weekend before Mom's arrival, we were visiting Father's family. Anticipating Mother's arrival, I was joyfully playing with my cousins. We girls were picking jasmine to make necklaces and bracelets. I jumped up trying to catch some blooms from the jasmine bush overhead and fell and landed on my arm. My elbow was twisted out of place. In agony, I hid myself, trying not to be seen by my aunts and grandma, to avoid seeing the doctor. I cried to God and asked Him to help me. I could not hide for long, though, and soon they heard me whining and took me to the osteopath. He forced my elbow into place. The pain was awful, but I was comforted by God's presence. I cried hard and was anxious for my mother's arrival.

The long-anticipated day arrived! Relatives gathered at Grandma's house. In keeping with the tradition, the cars traveled by caravan to the airport where we gathered on the balcony and waited for the plane to land. Then down to the luggage and immigration department we trooped and stood peering through the glass. My heart jumped for joy. Up and down I jumped, singing, "Mama is coming! Mama is coming!" *There she is, holding Maha's hand!* I charged through a cracked door. The guard saw me and the chase was on. He grabbed me and ordered me back. The area was restricted. "Please, sir, please, sir," I cried. "I need to see my mother."

A smile broke out on his face as he relented. "All right, little girl," and he took me to my mother.

Trembling with joy I cried out, "Mama! Mama!"

She in turn yelled, "Hino! Hino! My eyes and my life! I missed you." Up I jumped into her arms for loving embraces and kisses. "My, you have grown this year, my heart. Honey, I missed you."

"There, Mama, they are waiting anxiously to see you."

"How did you get in here?" she questioned.

"I sneaked in," I answered. As Mama was busy with her luggage, I took my sister and kissed her and squeezed her tightly. "Maha! Maha! I love you and I have missed you, Darling, come to me." She pushed me away and, in Spanish, asked Mother, "Who's she?" My four-year-old sister had forgotten me. She had been the "only child" and did not want to share her mother with another.

One by one, I removed my solid gold necklace, bracelet, and ring that Mama bought me before she left and tried to put them on Maha. She pushed my arms and flung the jewelry to the floor. In Spanish, she screamed, "Go away and leave me alone." The little fireball had thick jet-black hair, which bounced as she walked. Her frilly, feminine pink dress stood out to show her layered panties. "Leave my mommy. This is my mommy! She is not yours!" she screamed.

Although not understanding her speech, I sensed the rejection of one whom I loved so much. I was baffled.

Later that night at Grandma's, as we were preparing to retire, I whispered to Mother that I wanted to sleep with her. When Maha saw what was happening, she protested sharply. She yelled in Spanish, "Mamacita, tell that girl to leave." Mother gave in to her tears and urged me to wait until Maha could get used to me again. She assured me that another night I could sleep with her.

In a few days we started playing together. Maha spoke to me in Spanish; I spoke to her in Arabic. She called me "Hananita, Grandita, Amarita." Soon she returned to Arabic and we became close friends.

After a few months at Grandmother's house, Mother started searching for our own home. After many fruitless days, she settled on an old house in the middle of town. Just to be together again and in our own home was wonderful.

We helped Mother and the maid scrub the house and unpack the boxes. They cut lacy fringes from shelf paper to line the closets, shelves, and drawers. It took them days to finish the job. During that time many neighbors and relatives came to volunteer their help. It was such fun working together and listening to their chatter. They talked loudly, laughed, and expressed themselves with eyes and hands. How amusing to watch their outgoing and friendly personalities! And what a beautiful job they did of enhancing that old house!

We lived upstairs, with the storage and cellar downstairs. The courtyard and gardens were enclosed by a high rock wall and a gate that opened to downtown Schweifat.

Mother returned us to the International Evangelical School—a superior school academically and scholastically. Besides the regular studies, they taught three languages: Arabic, English, and French. The latter, an elective, I found difficult and begged my mother to have me excused. She did but regretted it later, since most of the people in Lebanon spoke the three languages.

The bus picked us up at 7:30 A.M. Maha was four years old, in kindergarten. I took her to her class every morning. In the afternoon, Mother or the maid met our bus at the gate.

What joy when we received Father's letter announcing his soon return to Lebanon. Dad had specialized in pediatrics at the Metropolitan Medical College in Manhattan, New York. Although he had been invited to continue there, he and Mother agreed that he should return home.

Across the valley, on a hill in a wooded area, a modern home was being built. It was surrounded with balconies and had large picture windows all around it. How delighted we were to be able to move into it—near many of our relatives! Frogs played around the goldfish pond, and two cats ate the field mice.

My cousin, Mona, lived near us. Walid, Maha, and I used to walk to her grandmother's home, where she lived. We played house in their garden, one of the prettiest I have ever seen. The fragrance of the freesia, tuberose, jasmine, plumeria, violets, roses, and carnations was unforgettable. Walid acted as the husband, Mona was the wife, and Maha and I were the children. We enjoyed the fancy dishes, dolls, and cookware that Mona's parents had sent from South America. Walid drove us all over in our homemade "car." We made tents with blankets and pretended we were camping. We also climbed to the roof of the house and sat under the grapevine shade of the pergola, where we made flower necklaces and bracelets. Time was unimportant, and we passed it leisurely.

After supper, we walked a few miles to the well—the village gathering place. We visited, quenched our thirst with fresh water, and returned home—skipping, singing, and thanking God.

We five appreciated the woods. Maha and I picked flowers and played with our pets while our big brothers hunted.

As Father's return drew near, Mother and the maids did a thorough housecleaning. The six big Persian carpets were hung in the sun for a week and beaten. Then they were vacuumed, shampooed, and again hung out in the sun to dry. The house smelled as clean as it looked!

A few days before my father's arrival, Maha developed a high fever. Mother took her to the town's old doctor, who was a neighbor and a relative. He checked her and gave her medicine for mumps instead of measles, and she got worst. Anxiously, we awaited Father's arrival. He was due on the morrow.

The boys had finished bathing. Mother was bathing Maha and me. The maid was making pita bread. Suddenly, the house shook. Things fell off the walls and cabinets. We all screamed. Mother helped us dress hurriedly. We ran to our nearest neighbor. Others joined us. We all stayed in the open field. Later, we cautiously reentered the house. An earthquake had struck; tremors continued. Again, I turned to God in prayer. Trusting Him, I slept.

CHAPTER III

Life with Father

❧

Father, aboard ship off the Lebanon shore, heard about the severe quake. He was worried. The next morning's evaluation indicated some fatalities, some injuries, and a few damaged buildings. We thanked God for our safety and prayed for the injured.

Relatives gathered at our home and, in a caravan, we drove to the Port of Beirut where Dad's ship was debarking. Even though I barely remembered him, I eagerly fixed my gaze on the ship's ladder. Mother pointed him out, and I ran to him. When he spotted us, his face shone from joy. Oh, the warmth I felt in my heart as I raced to him. I cried out, "Daddy! Daddy!" and hugged his leg and looked up to him. Giving me a wide smile, he pulled me up to himself and exclaimed, "Hanan! My Darling! My, you are quite a lady!" Touching his face, I declared, "Daddy you are so good-looking. You are younger than I thought." Laughing, he took me by the hand and together we ran to my mother and brothers. He took each one and ardently fixed multitudes of kisses on our cheeks, especially my mother's. What joy to be together again!

Grandma and Maha were waiting for us at home. Taking Maha in his arms, he hugged her affectionately, saying, "I am sorry, my eyes and my life, that you are sick, my darling. Don't worry. Daddy is here now. He will make you well."

"Yes, Daddy. I know you are the best doctor in the whole wide world."

More hugs, and then he asked for his fever thermometer and case. Impressed, we were confident that Daddy could make Maha feel better. He checked her out, looked at us, and announced, "She is going to be fine."

Smiling and nodding, we affirmed, "We're lucky to have a daddy like you to take care of us now."

He told Maha to stay in her bed while we all returned to the living room where the relatives were waiting. I jumped into his lap and every once in a while I felt his face with my hands, kissed it, and thought, *It's not soft like Mommy's, but I love him the same. What a Dad I have!* We feasted and had a jubilee.

After the guests left, we gathered around Maha. Daddy told us how thankful and relieved he was that we had been spared in the earthquake. He related stories of his long trip overseas and on the seas.

My brothers helped him bring in his trunks. Starting with Mother, he began presenting his gifts. For her, he had five elegant ensembles—complete with purses, shoes, and jewelry—and a gorgeous mink jacket. I tried it on, but it was so huge it swallowed me.

Then the watches! One for each of us. How delighted I was with my very first watch! Eagerly, I kept winding it. It broke. Grief stricken, I took it to Daddy who sent it to the jeweler's for repairs.

For Maha and me were identical gorgeous dresses from the best stores in New York; for the boys, a collection of fine suits. He didn't forget my cousins and grandma. Secure in Daddy's presence, we enjoyed many hours playing and talking together.

Vacation time ended, and Daddy rented a clinic in a high-rise building in Beirut. He decorated it especially for children. I loved visiting him, sitting in the waiting room with my sister and working the puzzles, building fancy block houses, playing games, and reading the colorful books.

Next on the agenda was purchasing a family car. Weekends, Daddy took us on family outings, often to the sea. We took turns riding on his back—hanging on his neck and hugging his waist with our legs so we wouldn't fall. Over the waves and under them, he would carry us. We also had tubes, and we floated with them to the shore. The quiet, clear blue Mediterranean felt like a big bathtub. Free of sharks and dangerous fish, it was wonderful! Together we built tunnels, houses, and castles on the sandy beaches. We used to lie in the sun for hours.

There I remember pondering, *Where is God? Who is God? My eyes have not seen God. My ears have not heard God. My hands have not touched God. My nose has not smelled God. My mouth has not tasted God. Why is He not revealed to me through my senses? I know He made me and my religion believes in these five main pillars. How I yearn to see, to hear, to smell, to touch, to taste of Him. I long to meet Him and to know Him.* My mind wondered again, and I remembered mother telling me, "God has always been there. He had no beginning and no end." *How can I understand that? I must be finite and very limited.* In my prayers and my spiritual self, however, God was real to me. He answered my prayers and drew me to Himself.

One day the school bus dropped Maha, Cousin Mona, and me across the street. Maha noticed our car parked near the house. Excited, thinking that Daddy was home, she ran in front of the traffic. A car struck her, throwing her across the street. Shivering with fear, I ran to her. I held her head as blood gushed out. I pressed on it with all my strength. I cried to God to help me and to keep Maha alive. Cousin Mona rushed to our home and called my brothers and the neighbors. Hurriedly, we took her to the doctor who checked her, cleaned her wounds and cuts, and did some stitching. He told us that she was fine and had only bruises and superficial cuts. How thankful I was to God! I praised Him for His reality in my life. We returned home and after a few hours Mom and Dad arrived. They were shocked to see Maha's head bandaged but were relieved to know that she was recovering well.

Our move to the capital was good for my father's practice. Beirut was a city of beautiful contrasts. Situated on a cliff with ravishing grass hills overlooking the sandy Mediterranean, its beaches caressed the feet of the city. A thriving cosmopolitan city, Beirut was filled with color of its exotic old and new—a city where the East and the West met in a melting pot of cultures and nations. How exciting it was to visit the outdoor cafes, boutiques, or grocery stores and hear many languages spoken, to rub shoulders with many different civilizations, and to have friends from almost every land. The surrounding streets near our apartment in the mazraa' subdivision were lined with boutiques and shops which displayed an array of tempting merchandise from Paris,

London, New York, Rome, and other cities. Next to it was a colorful souk and bazaar of a more traditional marketplace, which offered fresh fruit and vegetables, fish and meat, straw bags and baskets, ceramic pots and pottery from Lebanon and the exotic Middle East.

Even though our area was crowded with apartments and skyscrapers, a few blocks away mansions and villas with red-brick tile roofs were encircled by gorgeous breathtaking gardens, water fountains, and Greek figurines. We walked by them frequently en route to the beautiful huge pine forest park of Beirut, where children enjoyed playing and swinging in the fresh air.

Mother walked each morning to the market for her fresh fruit, vegetables, and meat; but she phoned for her groceries, which were delivered to our home. She spent her days with her maid preparing the meals and keeping an attractive home for us. At mealtime, we gathered around our fancy French steel, formal dinner table and listened to Daddy. He discussed medical information, Lebanese politics, world events, and many other subjects. We also were encouraged to talk and our dinner was a learning and teaching experience. Dad taught us that the world was at our feet, and we had a sense of openness to the whole world (just as the openness of our country in the center of the earth.)

Daddy moved us from the school in Schweifat to another American school, The Good Shepherd School, in Beirut. Being the school doctor, he visited the sick boarding students each morning, so we rode with him. We left at 7:30, and the school was half-an-hour away in East Beirut, on the steep hills of Ashrafieh. Afternoons we rode the school bus which went around Beirut before it arrived at our home. It was fun, but tiresome.

In that school we studied many subjects—languages, social studies, sciences, and maths. Life went smoothly for me during those years, and I excelled in school. I delighted in my studies and ranked with the top students. I was the teachers' pet and they all reported my progress to Daddy. I made some friends; but being the youngest in my classes, some were jealous of me and my achievements. I loved them anyway and refused to be intimidated. In fifth grade, I took the difficult government exam intended for the sixth grade. When I passed it with a high score, Daddy's buttons burst. I remember him telling me that he would like me to be a pediatrician and take his place when I grew up. I looked up to Daddy and enjoyed pleasing him.

In the summer, Daddy would take my brother Walid—his right hand helper—and me on the ambulance with his nurses. We traveled to southeast Lebanon, to Al-Arawan near the big Litani River, to the rural areas. Multitudes would await him. Doctors were scarce. Daddy would take free medicines and vitamins, give free checkups and medicine. I would hear them bless him and ask God to bless him and his family. Some of them gratefully brought him eggs, cheese, fruit, and vegetables from their farms.

My dad influenced me greatly and built my character. He loved the underdog and treated people equally despite their rank. He taught us not to be prejudiced and to love everybody. He was a humane person and money did not influence him. He knew that God would bless his honesty. In the building where he had his clinic, some dishonest doctors had agents at the bottom gate to entice patients to them. Others took commissions from drugstores and prescribed ineffective medicine to keep the people coming.

Daddy was known for his quick diagnosis and speedy results from the first few doses of his prescribed medicine.

My peaceful life was shattered by the turmoil of civil war in 1958. The Lebanese Army, with their heavy tanks and artillery, occupied the street in front of our home. Curious, Maha and I snuck out to the balcony. Helmeted soldiers yelled at us to go in. Quivering with fear, we ducked inside. For many nights we slept on the floor, wondering what the morning might bring.

As I saw and heard of people being killed in the streets and in their own homes, I praised God for protecting us. A bomb was planted beneath our window. Minutes before it exploded, it was discovered and dismantled. Again God intervened!

"Wafika!" called Dad to Mother as he dragged a bloody stranger into our normally immaculate home. "Bring me water and my case." As Mother responded, Dad answered our unasked question. "This man was shot by a sniper's bullet. He was standing right beside me!" Much as I pitied the wounded man, I thanked God that it was not Daddy. I was scared.

Two days later we raced to our car under a shower of bullets. Daddy sped to the town of Shweifat, where we stayed with Grandma until the war subsided.

My first personal encounter with death was that of a twenty-four-year-old relative—a member of the Druze resistance forces. The reality of it disturbed me and triggered my inquisitive mind. I wondered about life after death. My Druze religion taught me, "The soul and spirit will not die but will reincarnate into another human body until it is purified through different lives. When it is perfected, it meets its Creator and becomes one with Him."

Early teen years were spent on Hamra Street, the "Fifth Avenue of Beirut" and the artery of that western section. Gazing down from our spacious penthouse above the fourteen-story building dizzied me. A wide balcony with flower boxes and planters surrounded our residence. Besides the large formal living room we had a grand ballroom with the formal dining area adjacent with a powder room and lounge for guests. Next to the kitchen and family dining room were the maids' quarters, then four big bedrooms, each with its own bathroom.

That area of Beirut pulsated with *joie de vivre*. Hotels, cabarets, theaters, international restaurants, outdoor cafes, travel agencies, banks, and shops abounded. The rich, exotic culture of the East blended with the sophistication and luxury of the West. Night and day, strollers gracefully flaunted the latest fashions. The night was a social whirl festooned with a blaze of lights and filled with hilarious gaiety. Who could sleep with such activity wafting up to one's ears? But eventually one becomes accustomed to one's environment and we entered into the mood of Hamra Street.

Seeking tranquility, Dad took us to coastal towns and villages, to the mountains, and to the valleys. One morning in April we visited Byblos on the coast, north of Beirut. Cousin Mona and her three younger sisters and younger brother—who had all been born and raised in South America—came with their parents, Uncle Ramiz and Aunt Ekram, Mother's first cousins. The boys rode with Uncle and Aunt in their spacious, luxurious, maroon Pontiac, complete with chauffeur. We six girls preferred to ride in our big white Ford with Daddy because he was so much fun. We sang and clapped as we left Beirut.

Past the soft coral sea that bathed the beautiful sandy shores, we soon arrived at the Bay of Jounieh. We stopped to eat at its famous restaurant which, patterned after a Phoenician ship, extended into the sea. Mother called our attention to Beirut with its majestic setting on one side and gambling casino on the other. After we ordered the fresh fish of our choice, we rode the cable cars to the top of Mount Harissa to see the big statue of the Lady of Lebanon. The view was breathtaking. The entire town of Jounieh, with its beautiful red-topped villas and the blue sea shining in the sun, lay before us.

When we returned, our table was arrayed with hors d'oeuvres, samples of famous national dishes, hot fried fish, and beverages. Lebanese folk music was played in the background.

After lunch we proceeded to the beautiful Tabarja Beach which beckoned us for a swim.

On we proceeded to Byblos, an archeological site and the world's oldest continuously inhabited city. Traces of Phoenician, Egyptian, Assyrian, Roman, Greek, and Byzantine civilizations spanned six millennia. It was here that community living was first developed and strange gods worshiped. Early in the fifth millennium B.C., Byblos was already trading with Egypt, sending Lebanon's cedars through its ports for the construction of Pharaoh's funeral boats. In the thirteenth century B.C., the sarcophagi of Byblos' King Ahiram (mentioned in the Bible at the time of King Solomon) was engraved with alphabetic writing. The Romans left their monumental fountains and an amphitheater facing the sea. The crusaders' castle overlooked the evidences of the preceding civilizations. The warm sea breeze, the wildflowers squeezing out of the old rock crevice, and the vines hanging out of the castle windows added to the mystery of that ancient city.

Returning, we crossed a viaduct where conquerors from time immemorial have left their imprints along the river banks.

To escape the hot, humid Beirut summers, we delighted in excursions to the invigorating coolness and dry air of the Mount of Lebanon. Traveling north on the coast, we turned east near Jeita, where we visited its famous cave. After a mile walk, a boat took us into the heart of the grotto. We gasped with joy as the stalactites and stalagmites were suddenly illuminated with fascinating colorful lights. Our attention was lifted to a gallery where small orchestras were performing. Such magnificence stimulated my thoughts toward the majesty of the Creator of all. I was awed by His greatness!

For an hour we climbed the mountain, our backs to the calm blue sea. We moved inland toward the terraced mountains to Faraya, a quiet mountain resort. Our heavy sweaters felt good in the cool dry air. Near the spring and waterfalls, a small restaurant was located beneath the shady willows and poplars. Quickly, our tables were filled with *kebe* (ground wheat, crushed meat, onions, and spices), *tabouli* (a salad of finely chopped vegetables and cracked wheat), *kaftah mishwiyeh* (barbecued on skewers of ground meat with onions, parsley, and spices), and *shaworma* (mutton barbecued on a rotisserie). A basket overflowing with fresh cherries, apricots, grapes, peaches, and figs provided desert. As the adults drank coffee, we children danced to the Lebanese Dabkeh, folklore music. Everywhere we went, we made friends.

Besherre, our next stop, was the picturesque hometown of the famous Arabic Lebanese writer, philosopher, and artist,

Khalil Gibran. It was a thrill to visit the home of the Catholic writer of *The Prophet* and view his own paintings.

The Cedars, ten thousand feet above sea level, was a cluster of some four hundred cedars—the youngest more than a thousand years old (Ps. 104:16b). Winter skiers and summer climbers kept the chalets occupied year-round.

The steep, winding road down was scary. It was a relief to stop at the Kadisha Grotto, one of the valley's main attractions. Living in Lebanon and seeing all this created beauty spoken of in the Bible gave me a great appreciation for God. He captivated my thoughts! I enjoyed everything I saw and thanked Him for it constantly.

Another hot Saturday in July, we joined Uncle Ramiz's family for the drive to his hometown, the Mukhtara. At seven o'clock that morning we climbed into our cars. We passed Damor, the produce market center of Lebanon where handmade pottery was also sold. Mother and Aunt Ekram could not pass that temptation. They enjoyed bargaining and buying flowerpots of all designs and colors.

An hour later, we proceeded up the mountains. The sun shone relentlessly out of the pale blue sky. As we approached the summit, the sharp mountain air was dry and stimulating, the breeze fanning us as we sped along. What a contrast to the humidity of the coast!

Suddenly the two cars braked. Daddy stepped down to consult with Uncle regarding a breakfast stop. Various outdoor restaurants dotted the beautiful valley where two rivers and two mountains met. Our choice was at the foot of a mountain, under the shade of the umbrella pine, oak, poplar, and willows. The clear silver rivers meandered within reach of our tables.

A ruddy youth in his waiter's uniform cheerfully greeted us with his heavy mountain accent: "Welcome, Friends. The place is yours. Enjoy it and let me know when you are ready to order." The buzzing began as we ten children studied the menu.

The distinguished patron of the restaurant greeted us, using friendly gestures. His baggy black trousers and red fez set him off from the waiters. He discussed the place, the beauty of the setting, and the weather. "Take good care of these friends," he admonished the waiter as he beckoned him to take our order. Soon the table was filled with yogurt dishes, cheeses, butter, jam, and, of course, green and black olives. This was followed by hot grilled liver in a freshly baked pocket bread. Dad and Uncle Ramiz discussed politics over their thick demitasse Turkish coffee. Mom and Aunt Ekram compared problems with their maids. When we ten finished the hot *baklawa* pastry, we disappeared into the rocks and caves.

Playtime ended; our elders beckoned us to the cars. We continued up the steep mountains of the Shouf. The orchards and wildflowers fascinated me. I was attentive to not miss a thing.

Beiteddin, the magnificent nineteenth-century Lebanese palace and house of religion, was our next stop. Constructed of fine marble, intricate woodwork, and mother-of-pearl, it was a superb specimen of the decorative art of that period. Wide gardens beautified its entrance, which overlooked the terraced mountain slopes and valley.

Excitement mounted as we reached that dramatic Druze village of Mukhtara and Uncle Ramiz's colorful ancestral home. Pink oleanders surrounded the high walls and a pair of carved lions guarded the entrance. A marble well stood in the middle of the garden.

Aunt Monira rushed down the stairway. I can still visualize her beautiful smile and her rosy cheeks. Her light-brown hair bobbed backward under a snowy white veil. Her shiny aqua eyes welcomed us as she embraced and kissed each one. Joyously, she led us to the main courtyard under the grapevine roof, where the rest of the family and neighbors were awaiting us with sweets and beverages.

As the adults visited, we children sneaked next door for a peek at the home of our Druze civic leader, Junbulat. His palace stood on the hillside like a fortress with its terraced gardens and streams that ran through gazebos, rocks, flower beds, and stone caves emerging to the public waterfall where we spent our afternoon. A romantic outdoor restaurant secluded by a carved mountain formed the background for this waterfall, Ain Mershid, which gushed from the cliffs in cascades.

After dining there, the boys went horseback riding. We girls visited on the veranda. Townsfolk gathered to greet us. Kind, generous, and hospitable, these Druze people extended invitations to return and dine with them. Even the young Junbulat came with his bodyguard. He visited with Uncle Ramiz and cousins and left. Late that evening we returned to Beirut. How we enjoyed our summer days in the mountain.

CHAPTER IV

Adolescent Romance

℘

During adolescence I discovered a floating romanticism. My first fascination was for a lad a year younger than I. A glance at him activated the butterflies in my heart. I dreamed of him and longed for him.

But then I met Sami! When his talking green eyes met mine in the school bus, my heart was slain! Sami became my god! Never ever speaking with him, but still he dominated my thoughts and dreams. My eyes gravitated toward him in the schoolyard.

Druze culture condemned romance; the school forbade communication with boys. But Sami would visit my brothers, and I would scheme to get a glance at him.

Falling in love was equated with unfaithfulness. I made my choice. My attention was focused on Sami. God? I prayed to Him only in dire need. In His mercy, He responded. He foresaw the day when I would be wholly yielded to Him. He drew me to Himself. He created circumstances to enhance my need.

Gina, a Catholic girl, and popular singer, had been raised by her stepfather with what we considered loose moral values. At a party she danced all night with Sami. Although one of my closest friends who knew of my infatuation for Sami, still she gloated over her conquest. Deeply hurt, I lost respect for both of them; indeed, I lost faith in people.

Back to God I went with my supplications. He comforted my troubled heart, giving me temporary peace, mixed with restlessness.

Peter, son of a wealthy merchant, lived across the street. Our balcony overlooked his father's warehouse where Peter worked. Long hours I would stand in the sun on our balcony waiting for glances from him. Our eyes met and I was enthralled. But then I saw him with another girl and I despised him. Naively, I presumed that the slightest involvement must command total loyalty.

Samir, a Muslim from Tripoli, entered my life when I was sixteen, a senior in high school. His light brown hair, his eyes, his high intelligence captivated my heart. Lovesickness decimated my appetite for food or anything else. To prepare for his critical college entrance exam Samir retreated to his home in northern Lebanon. Of course, we had not communicated; so I knew nothing of his whereabouts. I decided he had forgotten me. Again I was downcast.

"Hanan, Hanan!" exclaimed my dear Muslim friend, Lina. "Did you see that good-looking Druze musician on the national TV? He has a cute American accent, and you should hear him sing!"

"No, I've never heard of him, and I'm not interested."

My enthusiastic musician friend continued to bubble. "He used to be a professional singer on the Lebanese radio in the fifties; he traveled and sang in Egypt; he played in an

Egyptian movie. Now he's a conductor and educator of classical music in the United States."

"Oh, good. So what?"

"His name is Bahjat Hamada," continued Lina, ignoring my disinterest.

"What? Hamada?"

"Yes, do you know him?"

"No, but I know his family. They are prominent Druzes. My uncle is married to a Hamada."

"Oh, Hanan, you should have seen him. He was so cute and impressive. I'd love to meet him."

"Good!" I replied in my bitterness. "Call the TV station and find out how to meet him. I have other problems. I can't stand another day without seeing Samir. What can I do?"

"I'm sorry, Hanan. I understand. But there is no hope in that relationship. Neither your parents nor his would allow a marriage into a different religion. Forget about him. In college you will have more freedom to talk with men. You may fall in love again."

"Lina, I can't imagine loving anybody else. Besides, I've not been able to concentrate on my studies, and I'm not doing well. I may never make it to the university."

Lina gently patted my back saying, "I'll pray for you."

Two nights later I was trying to study for my finals, but Samir dominated my thoughts. My books bored me and the doorbell signaled a break. Not waiting for the maid to open the door, I raced to see who was there. My parents were entering accompanied by two gentlemen. Mom winked and signaled with her hand that company had come. I was dressed casually in jeans. It was well versed in our traditions: When company comes, especially strangers, we dress for the occasion. Getting the message, I ran to my room. I sneaked a look at the younger of the two, without him seeing me. *He's a good-looking man. I wonder who he is?* I pondered.

Mom followed me to my room and informed me that I was to meet my cousin Mona's future fiancé. Soon my brothers and I, all properly dressed, entered the parlor. To my surprise, I was introduced to Bahjat Hamada. He seemed overwhelmed. We shook hands and I sat across the room. Contrary to my upbringing, he fixed his eyes on me and talked as if I were the only one present. He seemed to study me with his eyes. Jovially, he asked me to sit near him. We talked and laughed. He prolonged his stay. Daddy indicated it was time for them to leave.

"I hate to leave," said Bahjat, "but I must. It is getting late." As he was leaving, he squeezed my hand and asked, "What are you studying to be?"

"A medical doctor."

"No, I do not think you will." He talked with both voice and eyes. "I'll be seeing you again, soon."

Could this be my future husband? My heart beat fast.

I later learned that Bahjat had not slept that night. Rather, he had composed a guitar piece called "Hanan."

CHAPTER V

Engagement and Marriage

❦

Bahjat withdrew his proposal from my cousin and began visiting us daily. He fascinated me.In Father's clinic he appealed for my hand. Daddy expressed his love and his reluctance to release me, especially to allow one so young to relocate half a world away. He emphasized his concern that I continue my education. He concluded, "I do not speak for Hanan, though. I must talk with her; also to her mother and her brothers."

At dinner, Daddy related the conversation. He looked lovingly at me and said, "Hanan, you think about it soberly and let me know what you want to do."

I felt elated that Bahjat wanted me, but confused because Samir still dominated my emotions. I asked my sister to feel out my father and brothers regarding the possibility of marrying a Muslim. She reported the unthinkableness of marrying Samir.

For Bahjat, I lacked the passion I had for others. I admired him and responded to his flattery. He was the only heartthrob with whom I had been able to converse. I could be myself—not feel I had to put on or to fix myself to win his acceptance.

"Bahjat would be the best choice for me as a Druze," I reasoned. He was outgoing, good-looking, and educated. He was talented and a sensitive musician. He was popular and famous. He came from an aristocratic family. He had lived and traveled in many places. As a child he had lost both parents. I wanted to minister love to him. The adventure of traveling and living in America aroused my curiosity. The prospect of continuing my education also influenced my decision.

A few days later Daddy asked, "Hanan, what do you think of marriage to Bahjat Hamada?" He had talked further with Bahjat and trusted his word. "Bahjat would be a good, faithful husband to you, Hanan." He related all he knew about Bahjat and solicited, "What do you want to do? Do you want to marry Bahjat? Do you want to continue your education? Or both? Bahjat is willing to allow you to study after you marry him. Hanan, my love, this is your life. I do not want to think for you, nor do I want to influence you. Whatever you decide, you have my blessing."

Shyly I replied, "I would like to do both, Daddy. Bahjat is nice. I like him. He will be a good husband to me. But I would like to continue my education, too."

Daddy reported my decision to Bajhat and arranged for him to meet with Mother for details of the engagement, wedding, and dowry.

While I was in class, Bahjat visited Mother. They talked for hours but did not reach an agreement.

After school, I expected to see him. When I asked Mother about him, she evaded the issue. "We'll discuss it after dinner."

Puzzled and angry, I found solace in our young Syrian maid whose father had told her the history of the Hamada family.

"Bahjat's father was from a powerful Druze family in Lebanon," explained Akaber. "He was educated in France, so when the French took over Lebanon and Syria, the French felt they could trust him to rule for them and established him as the Prosecutor General of the mountains of Haran. Tenaciously holding to all he believed in, he ruled with an iron hand. This, the Syrian Druze resented. When Bahjat was a small child his father died suddenly. Within a few days, the baby sister also died. This left Bahjat and his older sister and brother. The widow and children returned to Lebanon.

"Having discussed the matter with your mother," she added, "I don't think your family is going to let you marry him."

Angrily, I isolated myself in my room and pouted. I would marry Bahjat no matter what! My brothers came to my room and tried to convince me that Bahjat could not provide the life to which I was accustomed.

"Living with him will be very difficult financially," they said. "Both of his parents are dead, and he has nothing. He has an older brother and sister. They are both in the United States, and I don't think they have much. You are too young to leave Lebanon, Hanan. You will be too far away in the States for us to see if you are living all right."

Disagreeing with all of them I declared, "I am going to marry him no matter what."

When Bahjat received my father's negative response due to his financial limitations, he left the city for the mountains. He phoned to talk with me, but Mother intercepted the call. He told her of an interview in one of the leading magazines which he wanted me to read. I did get the magazine and read it. In it he had a hint for me. His ideal of a wife was a description of me. For weeks we had no further contact.

My second cousin's wedding intensified my sadness. That night I dreamt that Bahjat and I had a beautiful wedding. In the morning I related it to my sister.

A letter from the United States arrived in my father's clinic. It was from Bahjat's unmarried sister. She expressed her concern for Bahjat's disappointment and emotional state. In many pages she discussed his qualities. She told of the dowry she had for me in the States, assuring Daddy of the excellent treatment they would extend to me. She promised help in sending me to college and sent an application for a school in Florida, where she was living.

Daddy shared the letter with us at the supper table. My parents and brothers admitted they had judged wrongly. Daddy sent a message to Bahjat to visit us again.

The formal engagement followed. A few of Bahjat's realitives came from Baakline and some of mine from Schweifat. I had designed my pink taffeta dress with pink ostrich feathers on the shoulders. Bahjat, handsome in his dark suit, joked and laughed. We both were ecstatic. His oldest uncle, the elder of his family, formally approached my maternal grandfather, who was the elder of my family. He asked for my hand and for the unity of the two families. Bahjat ceremoniously placed a wedding band on my right ring finger, and I, on his. He kissed me and we were formally engaged. The celebration lasted late that night.

Days and evenings Bahjat almost lived in our home. We talked incessantly. We sang together. He serenaded me at the balcony. How romantic! How beautiful!

During those days Bahjat opened up his life to me. His father's death had been caused by deliberate poisoning. A year later a multimillionaire who, with his family, had been servants to the Hamada family but who had relocated in America, returned to Lebanon to woo the widow, Souad. With plans to take her three children to America, Souad married her suitor. Immediately after the wedding, he reneged on his agreement and insisted on taking only his bride. He promised to send for the children after their honeymoon. A year later the three were still in Lebanon in the care of relatives and Souad was pregnant. The next thing they knew, their mother and infant brother had died in childbirth.

"When I went to America, I visited my stepfather who challenged me to work hard, to support myself. He counseled me how to get ahead in this new country. 'Change your name,' he advised. 'Take a name that everybody knows. Louis is a good name.' So all my friends in America know me as Louis."

"He handed me a shovel and said, 'Dig. That's the way I made it, and you must do the same.'"

"You mean, he refused to help you at all?"

"Exactly. He said, 'Let the one who brought you here take care of you.'"

"Who sponsored you in America?"

With a smile on his face, he told me about his older sister. "When Mother left Lebanon, Sister, who was fifteen, became everything to me."

"How old were you?"

"About eight. She made a home for my older brother and me. She was my security. She studied. She went to America and earned her Ph.D. at Chicago. She is so intelligent! She has written a book, and now she's teaching in a university in

Florida. After she got established, she sponsored my entrance to the United States. I'm indebted to her. You'll love her, Hanan."

Those weeks Mother, Bahjat, and I made frequent trips to the exotic souks and bazaars of Beirut to prepare my trousseau. For hours we meandered from shop to shop, diligently comparing quality and price.

First the fabrics! What fun to watch Mother bargain! A shopkeeper standing outside his door warmly greeted us, ushered us in, and served us cold drinks. Enthusiastically, with splendid gestures, he displayed his choice materials a bolt at a time.

"Have you ever seen anything like this?" Answering himself he boasted, "Of course not. There is none like it in all Beirut.

"Touch them. See for yourselves. I have nothing but the finest. The shop is yours. I am your slave and under your command. Tell me what you like and I have it."

Mother, playing her part well, acted displeased. The shopkeeper began swearing by his children and by himself to emphasize the truth of his words. Finally, Mother asked him to quote his price. Immediately she cut it by half. He then acted upset and shouted, "The shop is yours. Take it!" We made as though we were leaving. He called us back. They compromised until both were satisfied. Joyfully, he served us coffee. He cut the fabric and congratulated us for the sale.

For days the procedure continued. After the fabrics, the shoes. Then the cosmetics, perfume, and lingerie. Finally, the gold souk with all the exotic richness of the East. We studied the shops on both sides of that long mile.

A friend of mother's had a fine jewelry store. Because she trusted him, we did not bargain much with him. He fashioned my jewelry as I had designed it.

Eli Moad, a distinguished tailor was a graduate of a renown sewing school in Paris. I also designed my wardrobe, and he spent weeks preparing it. He charged over a thousand liras ($550) for his superb workmanship on each gorgeous outfit.

The elaborate wedding dress was made from exquisite lace, lined with thick silk satin. The shoulders were filled with delicate roses crafted from superb organdy.

He flattered my slender figure by offering me a job as a model. Besides being excited about my marriage plans, I disdained models: No respectable girl would be one!

The legal marriage took place in the home of Bahjat's uncle, the religious leader of the Druze. In the presence of my family and his, Uncle Rashid wrote the marriage license and prayed over us. Refreshments were served. The two families chatted.

The wedding still needed to be planned. Which friends, in addition to our five hundred relatives, would be invited? Professional associates would also have to be included. Many would come from a distance. Close relatives joined the deliberations. My uncle's enormous home would accommodate the ladies. Auntie invited the gentlemen to her grand two-story mansion next door.

On the wedding morning, Mother, Sister, my maid of honor, and I visited a French beautician who initiated me to the world of cosmetology. Next, the French hairstylist produced a head full of curls. How proud I was of my new image!

It was not yet noon when we arrived at Uncle's residence. The fragrance and beauty of tuberoses, carnations, roses, and gladiolus permeated the place. In the midst of the flower baskets, under palm branches, Aunt Nawal had placed her two "Louis the Fifteen" armchairs on a platform. Gifts overflowed the tables. Hundreds of chairs had been rented and filled the house and balconies.

The ladies of the family, who had come the day before to cook for the multitude, now served my family and close friends. According to the Lebanese custom, the groom and his family had not yet arrived. My mother, sister, and maid of honor accompanied me to a bedroom and assisted me in donning the bridal gown and jewels. They escorted me to the seat of honor. Guests began to fill the house. Every member of my tremendous family and all my friends hugged me, kissed me, and examined my jewels. This was our customary way of evaluating the status of the groom.

After all had greeted me, a messenger announced the coming of the Hamada family. Ceremoniously, my grandfather presented me to Bahjat, who removed my veil, kissed me, and took me from my father. He took his place by my side on the platform. Cameras clicked. Guests gazed. Bride beamed. Groom grinned.

With Bahjat on my right side and his cousin on my left, we waltzed out of the reception hall amid a shower of rice and flowers. A luxurious car, adorned with flowers, ribbons, and cotton was waiting to take us through the mountains, past resorts and villages, orchards, and gorgeous villas. The world receded as we dreamily skimmed between the clouds and the sea. A multicolored rainbow was cradled between two mountain ranges. A vast flowering plain was blessed with color. The red earth, the barley and wheat fields, the cherry orchards, the apple trees, and vineyards were nourished by the enclosing arms of the mountain ranges that forced the water into that luscious valley. Every green leaf and blade was blessedly fat. The blossoms perfumed the air. Snow covered the mountain peeks. Elated, we thought we were in paradise. The glitter of Beirut faded into a calm serenity and communion with love, happiness, and placid pleasure.

Delightful days were spent enjoying each other amidst the beauty of God's creation.

CHAPTER VI

Married Life in the United States

∂

To maintain his US residency, Bahjat needed to reenter the United States by September. We planned to settle in Maryland, where he had begun his master's degree program. After our two-week honeymoon we returned to my home. A month remained before classes at the University of Maryland would begin.

Awaiting Bahjat was a letter from his sister encouraging him to transfer to Florida State University (FSU) in Tallahasse, one hundred miles from her work in St. Petersburg, Florida. Her research had indicated that the music department at FSU was one of the five best in the country. He had to do this for our future, he explained, so I had no argument. A week before the wedding, I had applied for the American immigration permit which could take an indefinite period of time. His education was urgent.

Leaving me in the care of my parents, Bahjat flew to Florida. Dad began to get suspicious. Was there another woman in the picture? How reliable was this man?

A month later I was delighted to learn that my papers had been approved. My family bought my plane ticket, gave me money, and escorted me to the airport. The excitement buoyed me up, but when the gangplank was removed, reality struck this seventeen-year-old bride. I had been uprooted from my greenhouse environment. What would the future hold?

Jet lag. Strangers. Strange foods. Strange smells. Nausea. Foreign language. Interminable hours of travel. Fears. Would my husband meet me in New York? Dad had arranged for a cousin to meet me for backup. Tears flowed. My American seat mate offered comfort. He assured me that he would take care of me both in Paris where we changed planes and in New York. He admired my necklace and with comforting tones asked me confidential questions. Across the aisle a young American couple extended their sympathy. Although I had studied English (British English) their accent was something else! The couple and the older seat mate all exemplified a caring spirit. In Paris, the four of us non-French speakers stayed together, surveying the airport.

Joyous relief! Louis at the gate! Brrr! It was chilly in New York City. My "going away" suit wasn't warm enough. It felt good to be in the train en route to Washington, DC. Those colors! I had never experienced autumn splendor. How comforting to snuggle into loving arms!

The lights of the nighttime capitol overwhelmed me. Sightseeing from his friend's car that evening and the next morning impressed me with the majesty and greatness of this country. The flight to St. Petersburg, Florida, contrasted emotionally with the tiresome international flights.

The plane landed! Eager to meet my new sister, I proudly followed my husband down the aisle. There she was—short, stout, austere. She warmly hugged her younger brother (seven years younger, the only relative who had ever loved her since their mother's death twenty-five years before). Turning to me, she hugged me coldly and asserted, "Now *I* will take care of you!"

Cold chills ran through me. I felt her daring eyes analyzing me. Is this his *sister* or his *ruler*? Is she to be my parent, to govern me? What a contrast to my own darling parents—so warm, so caring, so trustworthy, but so far away.

Sister led us to her car and handed Louis (the name he had taken in America) the keys. She walked around and took her place next to him. Shocked, I meekly climbed in beside her. She escorted us to her office at the college.

"Hanan," she began, "Louis and you have a room in a home with an older couple. You're going to have to go to business school and learn typing so you can work and put Louis through his schooling." I listened in vain for mention of college and medical school for me.

"You cannot waste your time. You have to get the most out of your schooling."

A few days later Sister took me to enroll in business college. Louis, unemployed, was absorbed in television. Each afternoon he would pick me up and take me to her house, where I, the child, would be the "mother's helper." She would serve Louis like a king and then serve me a small portion. Afterwards I, the maid, did the dishes and the two of them would go into the living room and talk in French— their third language, which I did not understand. After the dishes, Louis and I drove home in her car which we parked ready for him to take me to class, then chauffeur Sister to her teaching position.

The following month, FSU accepted Louis into their combined master's and doctorate program in music education—on probation. Louis and I in our new car, and Sister and their older brother in his, made the day's trip north to Tallahassee where a furnished student apartment was awaiting us.

Brother stayed with us for a week and Sister a month in our tiny one-bedroom apartment.

"Louis," Sister commanded. "The bedroom door is not to be closed. Here I am, sleeping in your diminutive living room, and I need to go through your bedroom to get to the bathroom. Leave it open at all times."

Privately, in her diary she wrote: "Sex between spouses causes intimacy. *Let this never be!*"

During her month with us, Sister led me about the campus. She accompanied me to offices to inquire about job openings. She waited outside while I was interviewed by the manager of the comptroller's department of FSU, who gave me the job in the bookkeeping office.

"Sister, I am to start tomorrow morning at eight o'clock!"

"What did you do? Did you show them your figure?"

"No, of course not." I was humiliated by her assumption. Arriving home, I ran to tell Louis the good news.

Sister intercepted, "Yeah, she showed him her figure and gave him the eyes so he gave her the job."

Louis's countenance fell. His deathly stillness chilled me. Tension mounted throughout the month. Anticipation of Sister's flight home was my only comfort. But there in the airport, with voice accelerating in pitch and volume, she reprimanded him in Arabic for having closed our bedroom door the night before. She was enraged that we had had normal spousal relations.

Letters following her departure instructed us minutely. Each week Louis would go out to phone her. And each week, any progress we had made in our marriage adjustment was obliterated.

One year later, I had joyous news for my husband. Our first baby was on the way! Delightedly, he phoned the news to Sister. "How dare you not tell me before this happened," she exploded. "How can you afford to have children now?" The guilt she dumped on Louis pulled him further away from me.

A month before my due date, I quit my job. Mother came from Lebanon. We delighted in shopping for baby clothes and furniture to prepare a nursery in our new two-bedroom townhouse. What fun we had finding a second-hand crib and the new experience of refinishing it.

Due date passed. Thursday afternoon a hurricane warning was issued. We were instructed to tape our windows. The sky was pitch dark. Louis chose to leave the apartment. Ignorantly, Mother and I ineffectively taped the circumference of the windows. Torrential rains accompanying the hurricane gushed in through the air-conditioning opening, flooding the kitchen. Mopping the floor was a major operation. Terrified, Mother ran to the students next door. We got the situation under control and, exhausted, Mother and I retired. I was asleep when Louis returned.

In the wee hours of the morning, my water broke. Arising at six o'clock, I was embarrassed but Mother convinced me of the facts. Three hours later Louis drove Mother and me to the hospital. Omar was born at 1:30 P.M. Forgetting our troubles, the three of us were ecstatic over that wonderful son God gave us!

A few days after we came home, troubles reappeared. For a month, Mother endured the humidity, Florida heat (the air-conditioning opening had not been filled), and my husband's inhospitality. On a weekly basis he was being influenced by Sister, who was jealous of Mother. After each phone conversation with Sister, Louis's attitude degenerated. The physical plus emotional climate of the home gave Mother headaches. Brokenhearted and distressed about my situation, she begged me to return with Omar to Lebanon. My sense of loyalty overruled, and Mother left sobbing.

That year was filled with turmoil; but the omniscient, sovereign God sustained me. Summer 1967 was a time to rejoice! We celebrated Omar's first birthday and Louis's Ph.D.! Packing for his teaching assignment at Livingston University in Alabama was next.

Anticipating his first remuneration in our three-year marriage, we were excited about being financially free from Sister. We anticipated living happily ever after. Our expectations, however, failed. Her frequent letters, phone calls, and visits controlled our marriage. We had no chance to make it.

The cultural and commercial deficiencies of Livingston-plus-cow pastures failed to stimulate our cosmopolitan cravings. Louis's doctoral dissertation had developed a music program for Lebanon. He longed to apply the results of his study. He took steps toward trade in musical instruments and work in developing instrumental groups in Lebanese schools.

For my part, I felt that distancing ourselves from Sister might give our marriage a chance. However, I had mentioned divorce to Louis; and he figured that if there should be a divorce, he would get the better deal in Lebanon. There he would be awarded custody of Omar and would not have to pay me alimony.

A few days before our departure, a Billy Graham Crusade aired on television. Being under severe pressure, I was persuaded to listen to his message. Not fully understanding, I called the pastor of the Presbyterian church we frequented. "Pastor, would you come and baptize me, please."

"Why don't you wait until Sunday to be baptized in the church, Hanan?" he responded.

"Well," I replied. "You know, I am shy and I would rather do it at home, if it is OK with you."

"Of course, I'll come and bring the university dean and his wife tomorrow." The next day I was sprinkled in the presence of the two witnesses.

A few days afterwards I found myself with Louis and Omar on board the Olympic Airlines circling the Beirut Airport ready to land.

The Hamadas and the Hussians were behind the glass outside the Lebanese immigration. What joy when we had our first glimpse of them! Excitedly, forgetting our pains, we rushed into affectionate welcoming arms. My parents embraced Omar and proudly displayed him to all the relatives. The caravan proceeded to my parents' home. What jubilation!

A brief week of recuperation was filled with joyful reunions with family and friends. My parents gave us their bedroom; nothing was too good for us. In the soft nest of love, our second child was conceived.

The peaceful lull was short-lived. Sister appeared. It had been prearranged without my knowledge that she would spend her summer vacation in Lebanon. Louis and I met her at the airport and took her to a hotel. She demanded that Louis stay there with her. She would help him find our apartment and furnish it.

Outside my parents' home, Dad greeted us. In his presence, I mustered the courage to confront my husband. "Look, Louis, we came to Lebanon to give our marriage a chance. If you stay at the hotel, that's the end. I'll divorce you."

He countered, "OK, you're divorced." Dad was the witness and, according to our culture, that settled it. Louis entered and gathered his personal belongings and returned to Sister. Thereafter our home was closed to Louis.

Together they selected an apartment and traced family furniture which had been loaned to relatives.

CHAPTER VII

The Greatest Miracle in My Life

Ⅾ

It was the morning of December 8, 1969. I awoke depressed. I could not explain the weight on my shoulders. I had neither appetite nor joy. The children were fussy all day; still I carried out my chores. At dusk I nursed and bathed Sandy while the servant fed and bathed Omar. I kissed them and put them to bed.

At seven that evening Walid, the youngest of my three brothers, entered. Sensitive and considerate, he felt my need. After an encouraging hug, he asked me to dress—he would show me a great time. An hour later we were headed for Hamra Street, the "Fifth Avenue of Beirut." After parking his red convertible, we strolled along the narrow streets that were jammed with cars and people. Hamra Street was aglow with the twinkling lights of Christmas. The windows of the boutiques and shops were displaying the latest fashions and merchandise. A mixture of cultures and nations mingled in the street-side cafés. The air was filled with a variety of languages and music, perfumed with aromas of coffee, shish kebab, roasted chestnuts, peanuts, and corn. Everyone seemed happy and carefree, but I walked in a daze of misery and emptiness. It was not like me to be oblivious of my surroundings. As a teen, I had exulted in Hamra Street, watching people and admiring the elegant ladies.

That night, however, I walked like a robot; my mind was engrossed with God. Inside I was crying and in turmoil. As I gazed at the Christmas decorations, I wondered about Jesus Christ of Nazareth. *Was He really God in the flesh? If He really lives, can He help me?*

Walid was checking for a cinema I might enjoy. Startled, I noticed Louis and his bachelor friends sauntering by, chatting jovially. My heart was stricken with a sadness that brought tears to my eyes. I quickly brushed them away, hoping my brother had not noticed. Not wanting my husband to see me, I diverted Walid into a cinema where *Sweet Charity* was playing.

The heroine led a life of adventure and pleasure, yet groped for meaning in her life. She tried all that felt good but found only temporary satisfaction. Emptiness and despair overshadowed the conclusion.

I had wondered how these worldly women felt. They looked carefree and merry, enjoying everything the world offered to satisfy their egotism. Was life more satisfying for them?

Rebellion appealed to me. I would satisfy my heart's desires. I would rebel against my culture. I would reciprocate the hurt of my husband's mistreatment and the overprotection of my father and brothers. I would be free.

I thought of an unmarried school friend with whom I had lost touch during my years in the States. Unaware of her twisted growth of vanity, I had visited her in her fancy apartment near Hamra Street. Satan had painted a beautiful picture of her—she was happy, loved, and popular—I, miserable and lonely.

"Hanan," she had coaxed, "You are beautiful, but you are not appreciated. Leave Louis and you will be happy like I am. I'll help you meet the best people in Lebanon, and we'll run around together and have fun."

I had left her apartment struggling in a sea of self-pity and battered with waves of envy over the façade of free living. Now I pondered again her deceptive words, recalling how often I was tempted to call her despite my brothers' warnings to avoid her completely.

These memories, combined with the emotions evoked by the movie, caused my head to spin. I wanted to run and cry, burying myself beneath the bed covers. I needed space and time to evaluate my life and my destiny.

I did not then know why God protected me from her, but I now know He wanted me to be His and His alone. Because of His love, He was protecting my soul, wanting it to be unblemished and unscarred from defilement.

Walid was sweetly attempting to distract me with his wit and cajole me into a better mood. Despite his attempts, I remained withdrawn, preoccupied with questions about my being. Shattered under the weight of sin and the problems in my marriage, all seemed hopeless.

Eager to get to my parents' home, I went straight to my bedroom. Omar, three and a half, was asleep on the couch and Sandy, nine months, on my bed. Even as I had knelt as a carefree fourteen year old, by the same bed I knelt at twenty-one and cried out to the God of Abraham, the Great I Am, Allah (meaning, "God the Father"). I begged Him to help me.

I questioned Him and cried out with all my being, "God, who are You? Do You hear me? I know You created me. Please answer me, I beseech You. I'm going to stay here, awake, seeking You until You reply. My spirit is thirsty and hungry for You. Talk to me, dear God, I beg You! Are You an intangible force, or are You a personal God who cares? Who was that Christ who came so long ago? Is He really a manifestation of You, Your person, Your mercy, and Your compassion? Or was He a mere man? I want to know; help me to know. I cannot betray my religion, my culture, my heritage, and my identity unless I am sure. Satisfy my yearning spirit, O God."

Weeping continually, I recounted to Him my story as if to move the heart of my Creator. In those agonizing moments, I threw myself totally at His mercy. Distraught and exhausted, I collapsed.

In that state of emptiness and despair, God's spirit hovered over the chaos of my soul. Revealing Himself to me, He opened my spirit to His reality. His presence overwhelmed me. I saw Him as He is—a personal, compassionate God, the meek and loving Lord Jesus of Nazareth. My being was absorbed by Him as that pure, magnificent divine love showered and possessed me. He came to reside in my being, to give me a spiritual birth. His Eternal Seed took root in my spirit.

My soul found what it was seeking; I recognized my Creator—the Lord God of the universe, the Mighty God, the Prince of Peace, the Everlasting Father, the Lord of Lords, my LORD and my Savior, Jesus Christ.

He attracted me to Himself as He committed Himself to me. For the first time in my life, I felt love inexpressible. Then I saw myself as I am—selfish, bitter, rebellious, unworthy, and desperately lost. Overwhelmed by my helplessness, I searched, reaching for His outstretched arms. I had nought to offer Him but anger, fear, confusion, and weakness. He received me and cleansed my filthy heart as white as the snowcapped Mount of Sanin in Lebanon. He gave me peace and joy and healed the wounds of my soul as the balsam of ointment.

His presence illuminated my soul, preventing sleep. His loving blood flowed through my veins, consuming every sin. The Giver of Life became my life. He, the Giver of Peace, became my peace and my inexpressible joy. He said, "And you will seek Me and find Me, when you search for Me with all your heart" (Jer. 29:13).

My soul found its anchor in the presence of my beloved. What a happy, secure state! "The Lord has appeared of old to me, saying: 'Yes, I have loved you with an everlasting love; Therefore with lovingkindness I have drawn you'" (Jer. 31:3).

I arose the next morning rejuvenated; He had created in me a new heart. Now I am His follower and I can not be ashamed of Him. He said, "For whoever is ashamed of Me and My words, of him the Son of Man will be ashamed when he comes in His own glory" (Luke 9:26).

I sought Daddy to talk to him alone. Smiling and in a great mood, he was anxious to talk to me, too. He was concerned for my marriage, my children, and my life.

"Let's talk now," he said, and led the way into the parlor. "Close the door behind you, Darling. Have a seat here, Hanan, facing me.

"Hey, what is it about you this morning? You look rejuvenated. That Walid is a miracle worker! You both must have had a great time last night! Tell me what happened." With his full attention, he searched my face.

He was awestruck as I began relating my story in detail. His countenance changed as I proceeded. As I told him what God had done for me, I could see a look of disgust on his face.

"Christ is God!" I exclaimed. "He is the essence of God. He is the loving God. Dad, I know this as a fact. He visited me! He revealed Himself to me! I believe in Him, and I gave Him my life to control."

In shock, he listened to those words spoken with such conviction. "Hanan, you know you are under severe stress, and you are trying to find a door of relief. This is normal. I understand. But to believe such foolishness about a delusion—do you know what you are saying? You are demeaning and betraying your whole culture and religion—all that I have taught you. Hanan, you are deceiving yourself. What happened to you is not real. It is an illusion, a fragment of your imagination. You will get over it soon."

"No, Dad. It is not an illusion. It is the truth about God. Jesus is the express image of His person. He is going to help me. I know, for I am cleaving and trusting in Him."

Anger arose in his face. His voice intensified. "OK, if you want to be stubborn about this, take your kids and leave until you get your sanity. I do not want to see you until you change your mind about this craziness!"

Tearfully I packed our belongings, trusting God to handle the situation. *God will not deceive me. He will use even this to push me into reconciliation, and the future healing of my marriage. He will minister to the hurt in my father's*

82

feelings of betrayal and will reveal the truth to him at the proper season through His Word. "To everything there is a season, A time for every purpose under heaven" (Eccl. 3:1).

I returned to Louis in Ashrafieh, a new creation. I had a new meaning, a new hope, and a new reason for living. Now God was the source of my being; I depended not on my own resources.

My husband was bewildered. As the days passed, he knew I had been transformed. I shared my experience with him. I asked his forgiveness and together we gave our marriage to God.

Sunday came and he packed us into our small, beige Volkswagen, and we drove to a little church in Ras Beirut. As we entered, the wife of Louis's colleague saw us. She, Emiline Bush, broke out with tears of joy. She wanted to know all about it; and she wanted to know when I had met Jesus. We discovered it was at the same hour she had been on her knees, praying for me.

A week after my salvation, the Lord sent my way the head of Campus Crusade for Christ in Lebanon. He pastored one of the Evangelical Churches in Ras Beirut.

He, too, was excited about the love of God. "Hanan," he asked. "Do you know that God loves you and has a great plan for your life?" He opened his pocket Bible and asked me to read about it. "Put your name there, Hanan."

I read, "God so loved *Hanan* that He gave His only begotten Son that if *Hanan* believes in Him she should not perish but have everlasting life" (John 3:16).

"You know, we are born in sin and so are separated from God."

"Didn't God make man perfect?" I inquired.

"Yes, Hanan. God did make man in His image. Then do you know what happened?"

"No. Tell me."

"The first two people wanted to be like God. They weren't willing to obey Him but rebelliously chose to do their own thing. Their relationship with their Creator was broken."

"Look, Hanan, let me draw a picture for you. Here's a chasm. Man is on this side and God is way over on the other side. Sin brings death. Man couldn't get to God. But God actually loved us sinners. He gave Himself to be the bridge. Jesus stated that no one could get to the Father except through Him."

"Then Christ is our bridge to God the Father?"

"That's right, Hanan. Do you want to make a personal commitment to the Savior?"

"I did! Last week I met Him and gave Him my life."

We rejoiced together in that knowledge! Several weeks later, believers in Lebanon contacted Louis and me, inviting us to their meetings. One Bible study group met in a home on the top floor of a sky-rise apartment building. Mary Hollewel, another sister who had prayed for me, was there. Hungry and thirsty for the Word, we sang it, studied it, prayed it, and worshiped Jesus fervently. We attended every meeting, every church, every mission, and every Bible study we knew about. We met most of the followers of Christ in Lebanon. What joy!

We walked to a small Baptist church four blocks from our apartment every time the doors were open. Those believers sang vigorously. Passersby would hear us singing and enter out of curiosity. Their pastor was a blessing! I called him often to share the excitement of my discoveries of the treasures in the Word of God.

Every time I closed my eyes that week, it seemed there was an abundance of light within me. For months I buried myself in the Bible: I ate it, I drank it. My pleasure was to steal a few moments to be alone with my Savior and my God, whom I had hated, and who was my offense in my old beliefs. He had become and now is, *The Lover of My Soul.* It was He that my soul was created to enjoy and worship. Now He is mine. How happy I have become!

Nights passed like moments as I communed with the Father in prayer and meditation. Nothing could shake the profound peace He bestowed on me. Now, instead of arguing with my husband, I learned to go to my Source, my Heavenly Father, and ask Him to supply my need. He was always there to listen as I poured out my heart to Him. He understood the heart of a woman as no one else could. He always reassured me of His control of the situation.

One day a friend of Louis's called for a poker game. Instead of showing antagonism to Louis, as I once did, I took it to God. In my room, I dropped on my knees and asked God to free Louis from that bondage.

He left that night but returned in the early hours of the morning—miserable, depressed, and with his right hand aching.

Later that day, he confided in me that he felt sick inside. He knew that God was talking to him to stop gambling. He chose to obey the Lord. The next time his friends called for a poker game, he invited them to meet in our apartment. He hid his Bible beneath the blanket on the table. As they started to play, he surprised them with a Bible study. He explained why he was not going to gamble anymore.

Friends and relatives became offended because of the gospel. We were encouraged by Jesus' words, "Blessed are those who are persecuted for righteousness sake, for their's is the kingdom of heaven" (Matt. 5:10).

One of my special friends was an English lady, wife of one of Louis's colleagues. We planned frequent activities and visited regularly in each other's homes. She belonged to the Church of England, and I assumed she knew Jesus Christ as Lord.

One night at her home, caught up in the excitement of a party, I bubbled over, telling the group how God had given me meaning and hope in my life through Jesus Christ. Our hostess became incensed and ceased all communication with me.

We lost some friends and relatives, but gained more. On Easter Sunday we went up to the Rabieh, a ritzy summer resort in the mountains of Lebanon. The German Carmel Mission had a great Resurrection celebration for the body of believers in Lebanon. They were overwhelmed to meet a Druze couple in love with Christ. There we made new friends and felt a oneness in the Spirit. Our joy was full!

I began noticing God answering my prayers, both small and great. He drew me close into Himself. His love became my security and the source of my living. I witnessed His hand daily in my life, and for the first time I was not a prisoner to my emotions. I was free in spite of the circumstances. "If the Son makes you free," said Jesus, "you shall be free indeed" (John 8:36). My faith started to grow as I experienced practical lessons in which Christ built my character.

One night some of Louis' bachelor friends—journalists and show-business friends—threw a party in his honor in one of the Beirut apartments. Most of them were religious.

Although they did not smoke or drink, they reveled in entertainment of belly dancers and musicians. Dirty jokes and lustful talk permeated their conversations. The hypocrisy and pretense of virtue sickened me. I felt like a fire was burning within me. I wanted to get out of there.

I got up and asked Louis to stand for his convictions if he were a follower of Christ. I now realize my behavior was wrong; but in my immaturity as a Christian, I was not "wise as a serpent and meek as a dove." Thanks be to God, however, the Lord does not condemn us; but He will work all things together for good to those who love God, to those who are the called according to His purpose" (Rom. 8:28).

Louis angrily took me to my parents' home (where the children were) and returned to his party. It was late, and I was thankful that my parents were asleep. I did not have to explain why I came alone for the night. I went quietly to my room. Omar and Sandy were sound asleep. I knelt and talked to my Savior about proper behavior, controlling my anger and bitterness. I asked His forgiveness and His help.

In the morning the Lord led me to take a taxi to my new friend, Jackline, a mature believer. I saw the love of Christ in her eyes and on her countenance. She led me to her modest living room and we sat across from each other. After serving me hot tea, she smiled a wide angelic smile, as though I were the person in the world she wanted most to see. With compassionate care she asked, "What is troubling you, Hanan?"

With a broken heart I replied, "Here I am after just a few weeks of my salvation, failing terribly. I am acting like an unbeliever, even though I know with all my heart that what I stood for is right. I hate those parties!"

She explained to me the abiding presence of the Holy Spirit. She looked into my eyes and said, "Hanan, the Holy Spirit makes you hate what He hates. But Christ is meek and gentle."

She shared that the prophet Isaiah described Christ with these words:

He was oppressed and He was afflicted,
Yet He opened not His mouth;
He was led as a lamb to the slaughter,
And as a sheep before its shearers is silent,
So He opened not his mouth. (Is. 53:7)

Then she continued with 1 Peter 2:23:

Who, when He was reviled, did not revile in return;
When He suffered, He did not threaten, but committed
Himself to Him who judges righteously;

It is very normal, Hanan, for a born again Christian to hate sin. We need the mind and character of Christ to love the sinner." Lovingly, she added, "Hanan, do you love Louis?"

Surprised by the question, I blurted out, "Of course." We looked at 1 Corinthians 13:1–8 and read it together:

Though I speak with the tongues of men and of angels, but have not love, I have become as sounding brass or a clanging cymbal. And though I have the gift of prophecy, and understand all mysteries and all knowledge, and though I have all faith, so that I could remove mountains, but have not love, I am nothing. And though I bestow all my goods to feed the poor, and though I give my body to be burned, but have not love, it profits me nothing. Love suffers long, and is kind; love does not envy; love does not parade itself, is not puffed up; does not behave rudely, does not seek its own, is not provoked, thinks no evil; does not rejoice in iniquity, but rejoices in the truth; bears all things, believes all things, hopes all things, endures all things. Love never fails. . . .

As she shared this truth with me, I saw my love as selfish and conditional in contrast to God's way. I chose to love Louis with agapé love, sustained by God. Even my countenance blossomed as my soul was awakened and nurtured. Learning how to receive love, power, and life from the Lord's death and resurrection was exciting and awesome. I meditated on and learned from Isaiah 54:5–6:

For your Maker is your husband,
The Lord of hosts is His name;
And your Redeemer is the Holy One . . . ;
He is called the God of the whole earth.
For the Lord has called you
Like a woman forsaken and grieved in spirit,
Like a youthful wife when you were refused, says your
God.

In my new state of contentment in the Creator of love, it was possible for me to exercise a love that would not fail my husband. This was the beginning of my daily walk in my lifelong journey with my God.

CHAPTER VIII

Life in New York

☙

March 1971 was a trying month in my life. After bathing Sandy and putting her to bed on March 3, I began undressing Omar. Small, pinlike bruises all over his back alarmed me. "Darling," I said, kissing him, "Do you hurt, my sweetie?"

Perking up, he answered. "No, Mommie, I am fine." I put him in the bubbly warm bath and left him with his rubber toys to play.

After his bath, Louis, Omar, and I knelt by the side of his bed to talk with our dear Lord Jesus. The four year old tugged on my shirt, saying, "Me first." He closed his beautiful little eyes "Jesus," he prayed, "I love You. Thank you for You, for Daddy, Mommy, and Sandy. Give us a good night sleep and let Your angels take care of us. Good night, dear Lord. Amen."

We tucked him in and showered him with kisses. Reaching to me, he pleaded, "Please tell me a story." Perched on the edge of the bed, I rubbed his head and put him to sleep with a story.

In the morning, I called the pediatrician to report the bruises. He informed me, "Unless Omar has a fever, Mrs. Hamada, don't worry."

Louis's two years as professor of music with the Beirut College for Women had been fulfilling. He had organized bands there and in two other schools. But because of some foreign political infiltration which Louis had opposed, his teaching position at the college had been terminated. At about that time, Sister became aware of a one-year sabbatical opening in the music department of an elite public school on Long Island.

The Garden City High School winter concert was scheduled for one week after the onset of Omar's symptoms. It would be a highlight in Louis's career. We would leave Sandy with the baby sitter. That week Omar's bruises had enlarged and multiplied, but no fever.

As we were dressing for the concert, I noticed Omar's bloodshot eyes. Frightened, I cried out, "Honey! Look at his eyes!" Examining the child, he announced: "We're taking him to the doctor *now!*"

Omar, in his Sunday suit, and Louis and I, in formal attire, rushed to Dr. Horowitz. "What seems to be the trouble?" he questioned.

"Omar is bleeding internally, I think." After examining the eyes and bruises, he summoned three more doctors. The unanimous opinion: Admit him to the hospital for a leukemia checkup.

With tearful eyes and in semishock, Louis and I drove him to the hospital. We submitted our baby to God and to the hospital staff and proceeded to the concert. Louis escorted me to the auditorium, then rushed to his office. Closing the door, he knelt and sobbed, "Lord, if you heal my son . . . in the next concert, I will magnify and glorify Your Name. I will tell about You."

Arising, he washed his face and went to the stage. His waiting students, moved by his red eyes, asked what was the matter. "Omar is critical." No time for explanations; the rehearsal must proceed. Music lovers were filling the 1,000-seat auditorium. It was eight o'clock and the beautiful classical music began. Louis, with eyes too blurred to read, conducted from memory. From the balcony, I marveled at God's intervention: The orchestra played with superb smoothness. Applause was generous and a long standing ovation climaxed the grand finale.

At home we silently prepared for bed. Feeling torn inside and helpless, I dropped on my face and desperately prayed, *Help me, Lord God. I don't know what to say or how to pray but I ask Your grace to be sufficient for these awful moments of my life.* I opened my Bible to Isaiah 30, verse 19, and read, "He will be very gracious to you at the sound of your cry; When He shall hear it, He will answer you." Eventually, I slept. Food disinterested me and sleep evaded me for a week.

"Omar has a rare type of blood disease, Idiopathic Thrombocytopenic Purpura," reported Dr. Horowitz. "His platelet count is dangerously low. His blood is not clotting and he is bleeding internally. Since you said he was in contact with the chickenpox virus, we can't administer cortisone; his body can't handle it." For a week, we waited.

During that severe trial, God taught me through His Word. I learned to submit myself to the Lord without reservation. Though it seemed He had left me for a while to exercise my faith, yet He never failed me. My need was desperate; I learned to cast my "care upon Him for He cares for [me]" (1 Peter 5:7).

March 18 we passed through the valley of the shadow of death. Omar's platelet count plummeted, the bleeding became extensive, blood vessels in his brain hemorrhaged. Death was imminent. Louis and I told our four year old about his condition. We talked to him about Jesus, heaven, and hell. "Do you want to give your life to Jesus? He said, 'Let the little children to come to me . . . for of such is the kingdom of heaven . . . '"(Matt. 19:14).

After we left, he asked a nurse to read to him Matthew 5. After she left, he closed his eyes and said, "Lord Jesus, I give You my life." During the night he had a dream that the Lord Himself touched his body. That same night, Louis and I, on our faces before God, agreed in earnest prayer. Feeling shattered with pain, we alternately prayed, questioned, wept, and prayed some more. *How can such a terrible thing happen to us? Is it necessary for God to punish us for some sin? Something we don't even know we've done? Why should this be? Why?*

We prayed that God would spare Omar's life. Yet we were willing to accept God's perfect will for our son—no matter what it may be. It was the hardest thing we had ever done. Nevertheless, with tears, pain, and eventual victory, we surrendered Omar to God. We comprehended for the first time the bitterness of the cross and the actual love of God. At last, I laid back on my pillow, drained. I slept soundly. I dreamt that the Lord Jesus touched Omar and healed him.

Early in the morning the phone interrupted my dream. Dr. Horowitz greeted me: "Mrs. Hamada, good morning. Omar's blood is normal this morning, and his platelet count is above average. This does not mean that it will not drop suddenly again," he warned, "which is common with this disease."

"Dr. Horowitz," I replied. "Omar is fine. His platelet count will not drop again. Jesus touched my son and made him whole."

"OK, Mrs. Hamada. I just thought I'd tell you the new development."

The nine months since we had returned from Lebanon, we had been living on Long Island, New York—a fifteen-minute drive from Sister, who was teaching anthropology and marriage-and-family in a local university. Her daily visits continued to threaten our marriage. Omar's illness exacerbated her harassments.

"You—! Because of *you* he is sick! You don't take care of him! You let him play with those children with chickenpox! You should keep him in the house with you. If you weren't so busy (blah blah blah), you would have been watching him!"

God used this instrument of spiritual surgery for my growth. Through this internal anguish and purging, He drew me to new depths into Himself. Yet His Word—the Bible—and His people—members of the New Hyde Park Baptist Church—undergirded me. Pastor Jackson stood by us, encouraging us and comforting us. He faithfully visited at the hospital.

"Pastor, I'm finding security for my soul in God's Word. In spite of my worry over Omar and the frustration of Sister's accusations, God is giving me joy for my spirit. Look at the passage God gave me:

> But now, thus saith the Lord who created you . . . And He who formed you, . . . "Fear not, for I have redeemed you; I have called you by your name; You are Mine. When you pass through the waters, I will be with you; And

through the rivers, they shall not overflow you, When you walk through the fire, you shall not be burned, Nor shall the flame scorch you. (Is. 43:1–2)

"That's from Isaiah 43, isn't it? Hanan, the whole church has been praying in one accord for Omar's life and for your marriage. Anyone else would have been on drugs, would have run away, ended her life, or been committed to the mental hospital. We are very proud of you, and praise God for you."

"Thank you, Pastor. I could not have stood alone. That precious Joanne Hornish! Taking my chickenpoxy baby into her home with her four children! And then they *all* got chickenpox! Sandy wasn't yet potty trained! And I couldn't even visit her for fear of carrying infection to Omar! What a blessing Joanne has been to me! The others, too! All those cards, notes, and assurances of prayers! God has loved me through your church. And, 'His grace is sufficient for me.'

"Look at what God showed me from 2 Chronicles 16:8–9:

. . . because you relied on the LORD, He delivered them into your hand. For the eyes of the LORD run to and fro throughout the whole earth, to show Himself strong on behalf of those whose heart is loyal to Him. . . .

For a week after God's touch, the doctor kept Omar under observation. What a contrast he was to the young leukemia patients! Playing in the game room, he regained his strength and was eager to return home. What joy when I could bring my perky youngster home! The next day Sandy, free of contagion, joined us! How wonderful to have the family together again!

Two months passed, and Louis was preparing for the Spring Concert. He remembered his promise to God. Sister demanded that he consider his position and not make a fool of himself. "You will offend this community! Keep your preaching in the church! You're here to conduct the orchestra! They'll fire you!"

Louis struggled. He had listened to Sister many times before. But now his conscience pricked his soul. He had made a pledge to God. God had performed a multiple miracle—the eternal salvation of his young son's soul, Omar's dream and assurance of healing, my confirming dream, all this followed by the healing of the child whom the doctors had relegated to the grave.

Day by day his students tracked Omar's progress. They rejoiced with their director over his son's healing. Tomorrow would be the Spring Concert.

"Danny," he said, "tomorrow night, at the beginning of the concert, I want you to bring my son from the front row to the stage."

"Great!" responded Danny. "You show 'em how God healed him."

Saturday, Louis asked me to dress Omar for the stage. He had reserved seats for us in the front row.

The curtains opened. After the first selection, Danny descended from the stage. Omar enthusiastically accompanied his friend, eager to participate in relating God's gracious healing. Proudly he grasped his father's hand. With a smile directed up to him—the biggest and most important man in the world to this strutting youth—Omar waved to the audience. Louis related his odyssey with God: his own salvation, his wife's salvation, Omar's salvation followed by that miraculous healing. Greatly moved, the audience applauded with a standing ovation. God was glorified!! Only Sister and her companion were mortified.

> Blessed be the God and Father of our Lord Jesus Christ, the Father of mercies and God of all comfort, who comforts us in all our tribulation, that we may be able to comfort those who are in any trouble, with the comfort with which we ourselves are comforted by God. (2 Cor. 1:3–4)

CHAPTER IX

California

⳥

L ouis's position in New York, filling another director's sabbatical leave, came to an end. Where
to next? We sent résumés to scores of colleges
throughout the United States, starting on the East Coast.
Eventually, Dr. Angelica responded with an invitation for
Louis to fly across the continent for an interview. This gracious lady, proprietress of a growing, full-scale religious
institution from kindergarten through college level, welcomed him enthusiastically. After a tour of the facilities,
she introduced him at an informal reception. He was impressed with the housing that she showed him, next to the
campus. She knew that his wife would want it redecorated
and assured him that her wishes would be honored—new
carpets, new curtains, fresh paint, new appliances.

Although the distance was formidable, advantages of climate, some favorite relatives, and escape from Sister com-
pensated. We moved in July and had a month to settle in.
The whole situation was beautiful—mild weather reminis-
cent of Lebanon, with flowers, fruits, and smells so familiar;

proximity to the sea; and even a favorite first cousin, Caleb, with his lovely American wife, Mary. A mutual first cousin to Caleb and Louis had been a clinic partner with my father; and Caleb had often visited the clinic, as well as our home. He regaled us with stories. What a delight to vacation with these hospitable folks.

Soon our first decent-sized accommodations since living in America were ready—my first house! Dr. Angelica had directed the students to follow my color choices. Although the house was old, it was clean, comfortable, and cozy.

Classes began in August. Louis was responsible for all music instruction from first grade through college, some five hundred students—classes, orchestras, choirs, including some members of the large church which Dr. Angelica pastored. An active schedule of performances kept him on his toes.

I delighted in Dr. Angelica's classes—my first formal Bible training! Daily all-campus chapel and church services were exciting: Miraculous healings took place, prophecies were given, tongues with interpretations were common, worshipers communed with God in English as well as in supernatural tongues, and testimonies challenged her followers. Never had we heard such dynamic preaching! Emphasis included salvation, healings, the necessity of speaking in tongues, submission, and obedience.

Omar was placed in kindergarten and in a month moved to first grade. He loved the school and the challenge. Our new friend, Ingrid, being financially independent, offered to care for Sandy while I was in class and during my prayer and study times.

"Thank you so much, Ingrid, for your loving care for my children."

"They're like my own, Hanan. They fill my life with joy."

"Ingrid, you know Louis is going to that music convention for a few days. But I won't be lonely, because I really want to spend this time with the Lord."

"Hanan, you *know* you could never devote yourself to prayer and fasting while keeping up with those two kids! Let me take your active little darlings! I'd *love* to!"

What a rich experience to be shut up with God with no family interruptions! "God," I prayed, "I want to know You, I want to be intimate with You; I want You to fill me with Your Spirit." I had been inspired by reading both the Bible and stories of the lives of great Christians.

"Bless you, Ingrid! How can I thank you enough for allowing me this wonderful time with my beloved Savior!"

"Oh, Hanan, it was a joy having Omar and Sandy! We had such fun! They kept me going!"

"Ingrid, let me tell you what the *Lord* has shown me— to seek the Giver, alone and not the gift. God is the object and aim of our adoration, and not the gift.

"The Lord overturned my temple that I have tried to build by human endeavors in order to build a divine structure—one that is not built by human hands, but an eternal one! He showed me the secret of His incomprehensible wisdom, which is unknown to any besides Himself. Who am I to know His mind? Look at Isaiah 55:9.

> For as the heavens are higher than the earth, so are My ways higher than your ways, and my thoughts than your thoughts.

"Isn't it wonderful, Hanan, how Dr. Angelica is inspiring your life?"

"Yes, but, Ingrid, yesterday I gave myself as a temple, consecrated to God for time and eternity. He is residing in me. He is preserving my spirit for His use."

"Oh, that's awesome!"

"Yes, His kingdom is within me. I personally experienced Him as the King of Kings! He reigns supremely within me to do His will. Ingrid, let's look at John 14:23 together.

"If any one loves Me, he will keep My word and My Father will love him and We will come to him and make Our home with him."

"It is great to have you here with Dr. Angelica as part of our family."

Louis entered our *tête-à-tête*, enthusiastically reporting on the music conference and his ideas for his winter concerts.

"Welcome home, darling! I had a great time, too. Because of Ingrid, I was able to spend time alone with God. I can't wait to tell you all that I have experienced."

"We love you, Ingrid. You are part of our family."

It was good to be reunited as a family.

"Hanan," said Louis. "You go ahead to the meeting tonight. I'll put the children to bed. I have to organize my notes and my thoughts."

Eagerly, I joined the worshipers in the 2,000-seat auditorium. As I listened and observed, my spirit was troubled. *Who* is being glorified here? I listened to the testimonies. *Praise you, Dr. Angelica! . . . Since you prayed over me, my life has not been the same . . . I was healed last week by your touch!* I listened to the message. *We have been persecuted for Christ's sake! My husband died in prison for his faith. We praise God for His anointing on our family.* And again, *God is pleased with obedience and submission. God's word says, 'Touch not*

*mine anointed, and do my prophets no harm.' God will bless
you for your obedience, for your submission.*

Louis, too, was experiencing frustration. "What went
on in chapel today, Hanan? The next class was half-an-hour
late."

"Oh, Louis, I'm afraid she's accepting worship. Students and staff queued up to report the awesomeness of
her ministry."

"She is a dynamic, charismatic preacher! But it really
fouls up my lesson plans when the after-chapel class is cut
short."

The Christmas concert was a great success. The orchestra, harpists, and choir performed beautifully. It had been
widely advertized and well attended.

Dr. Angelica brought Christmas presents: a small violin
for Omar and a beautiful doll for Sandy, took pictures with
the children, and showered her love on them. How happy
this made me!

In January, Louis came home one day, agitated. "That
son of Dr. Angelica is a pain in the neck! He's constantly
contradicting me in class. He wants to be the final authority. You should see the faces of the students if I disagree
with him."

"What did he do?"

"He stood up and challenged my authority. I pointed
my finger and commanded, 'Sit down, Boy!'"

"Louis, how could you? He's taking after his mother
and is being groomed to take over the school someday. You
might eventually be working under him."

Another day Louis exclaimed, "You'll never believe this,
Hanan. Dr. Angelica called me down for reprimanding her
son. She insists he is the authority in the class. I can't work
in a situation like this!"

"Honey, please! You've just started! We can't pull out in the middle of the year. How could you break your contract with her? What will we do? This is the best place we've ever had to live. And I love California. Omar loves his teacher and he's progressing so well. For the first time in America we have a family that cares. Dr. Angelica has done everything for us. Ingrid, too, and the whole church and school!"

Louis bit his lip and continued. He felt uncomfortable sitting under her preaching but encouraged me to attend.

With TV being outlawed by Dr. Angelica, our contact with the outside world was radio. Harold Camping, on Family Radio, appealed to Louis. We had enjoyed his "Open Forum" while we were in New York. His teaching alerted us to possible cult connections. Now we realized that his headquarters was near our home. Louis called for an appointment, which was immediately granted. Mr. Camping strongly exhorted Louis to remove himself and family from this organization, that it is a false cult. Pressure to kowtow to the son ceased.

Sunday we attended church together. For the first time we noticed a seal over the inner door. A woman, sitting on a throne with a crown on her head held a cross in her hand. Clearly, this woman was Dr. Angelica. Our eyes were opening.

Visitors and "outsiders" rarely spoke against God's anointed. "I warned him," she said. Tears came to her eyes. She had been faithful in admonishing him. "But he didn't listen. He left our fellowship. He went out into the world. I had to wash my hands of him. It was God who dealt with him. A horrible auto wreck sent him to the hospital, and he was left as a vegetable. It's *you* I'm concerned about. Yield yourselves to the authority that *God* has placed over you."

She pleaded with those who were walking in rebellion to come forward for repentance.

Louis and I looked at each other. We knew she was talking to us. We felt trapped like two little mice in a corner.

The next week she summoned Louis to her office.

"Hanan," exulted Louis when he returned home. "Free at last! Free at last! Praise God, Almighty! We're free at last!"

"What are we going to do? What about Omar's schooling?"

"It's me she's mad at, Hanan. Not you. You keep going to her church, and then Omar can stay in the school. I'll start looking for another position."

"In the meantime, I'll look for a job."

"Hanan, how about our going to Africa as missionaries?"

"If God wants us there, I'll go with you, Louis."

"I'm going to write to foreign mission boards."

The mission boards unanimously rejected us. Louis was too old; neither of us had graduated from a Bible school or seminary; we had not had two years of practical Christian experience; we had no church membership or recommendation from a pastor.

Five more months we stayed in the house. Omar completed first grade; I got a job as bookkeeper; Louis did research on possible openings for him; and I typed letters to send with résumés. Ingrid cared for the children while I worked. From 450 applications, two favorable responses came, one from Jackson, Mississippi, and the other from Jackson, Tennessee. The situation in Mississippi appealed to me. But Louis flew to Tennessee, visited the all-black campus and called home. "Hanan, I've found my Africa in the United States! We're coming here. Get ready!"

After Dr. Angelica dismissed us, we gravitated toward the high school principal and his schoolteacher wife, who had become uneasy about the climate of the school. John collaborated with Louis in a research of Dr. Angelica's life, finding many inconsistencies. Joann and Ingrid supported me emotionally as together we packed and closed our house.

As Ingrid took the children out for a walk, Joann and I talked and packed. "Hanan, knowing the Lord, I know that this year wasn't wasted. He must have taught you a lot, spiritually."

"Yes, of course. In 2 Corinthians 11:14 Paul shows that Satan transforms himself into an angel of light."

"Aha! This is generally the case with those who are seeking spiritual ecstacy."

"It is a spiritual adultery and sensuality for the soul to enjoy the experience and not the Giver."

"You're right, Hanan. The enemy entraps the soul which is filled with vanity and self love, hindering it from worshiping the Lord Jesus exclusively."

"Joann, I've found that the revelation of the enemy takes our eyes away from Jesus Christ and hinders us from dying to self."

"But Jesus' revelation to the soul through His eternal Word makes us a new creature in Him."

"Joann, I believe that when we attach ourselves to any gift we, lose the real enjoyment of the Giver. The soul should be lost in God. Someday as our souls will be glorified in Him, we will be hid with Christ in God. Hallelujah!"

CHAPTER X

Tennessee: 1973

℘

An air-conditioned room welcomed us in the Winslow, Arizona, hotel at the end of two days of driving through Death Valley with two half-baked children. After bread and cold cuts, washed down with warm coke in the oven we called a car, we enjoyed a real, sit-down restaurant meal. Baths and beds with fresh linens felt like heaven.

Midnight arrived. Louis had an emergency and went into the bathroom.

"Hanan, I think I'm having a heart attack!"

"I'll call the desk. We need an ambulance!"

"Hanan, it's Friday. Dr. Angelica is having her all-night prayer meeting."

"Louis, she threatened that if we left, tragedy would strike."

"Hanan, pray!"

"May the Lord rebuke you, Satan! I plead the blood of Jesus! Please, Lord, I beg you, to touch my husband and heal him. In Jesus' name. Amen."

The paramedics were at the door; Louis was whisked away; I was left with the two frightened children. Together we clung to the Lord's promises.

Thirty-six hours later we resumed our journey! How the Lord had answered prayer!

"Could you believe it, Hanan?" said the sole driver of the car. "Both the doctor and the nurse were Christians! They prayed for me."

New Mexico, Texas, Oklahoma, Arkansas. We could at least see Tennessee on the map! Desert and mountains gave way to monotonous plains and torrential rains. "Hanan, I can't see the road!"

"Can't we stop in a motel? The kids are impossible." A neon sign suddenly appeared: VACANCY. Without hesitation, Louis turned in. Anything would be better than this blind driving.

"Spiders!" screamed Omar, with Sandy echoing his cry. "Daddy, I don't want to sleep here!"

"Thank God, we're in out of the rain! Get down on your knees and let's express our gratefulness to God for protecting us on that road." And God *did* protect us both on the road and in that insect-ridden motel room.

A few more hours and our weary foursome drove up to the newly built complex where Louis had rented an apartment.

We were excited about Louis teaching in a Christian institution, Lane College (LC). He wasn't aware that the students reveled exclusively in black soul music. The resistance to his classical music formed a wedge between him and his students. In his music-appreciation class he related God's creation to the three elements of music: rhythm, melody, harmony. He took them into the book of Genesis as the source of music, and from there to salvation.

Louis was not prepared to find that, although LC was church related, a minute minority of the staff and student body were Christians. He also was prepared neither for the resistance nor rebellion against Christianity.

"I'm going to wipe that smile off your @$#* face," growled a bear of a student in class one day. Louis sent up a silent prayer, and watched as God sent the student to his seat.

"I want to see you in my office at 2 o'clock today." At that appointment, Louis learned that these students had been brainwashed into believing that Genesis taught that blacks were second-class people—cursed by God after the flood because of Ham's sin. No wonder they resented Louis's teaching.

Mr. Ed McAteer, a Christian businessman, worked with a few pastors to bring Dr. Adrian Rogers for a racially mixed evangelistic crusade in the Jackson Coliseum. Mr. McAteer was aware of a Christian professor of music at LC and contacted Louis, asking for his help in arranging a meeting in the main auditorium of LC. We were thrilled and cooperated fully. To the surprise of the black student body, many whites attended. After a powerful message from the Word of God, many students responded to the invitation to accept Jesus Christ as their Savior. The atmosphere was charged. Repentant students were sobbing.

As we left the service, we were grieved to hear a campus leader exhorting the students: "You're not going to follow no white man! You can count on it! He ain't telling you no truth!"

Few of those who made a commitment to Christ followed through with Bible study and a godly life. Louis was unaware of any strong Christians on the faculty or in the

109

student body. All this frustration drove him to the Bible and, eventually, to Dallas Theological Seminary where he took correspondence courses and attended classes during every vacation time. He wrote his thesis on "The Curse," and then was able to explain that the curse was on the land, not the people. The door was opened for him to draw his students to Jesus Christ, a group of whom began meeting with us on Wednesday evenings to learn about the love of God and on Fridays to study the wrath of God—a balanced diet. (Twenty years later he was blessed to meet some of these students at Dallas Theological Seminary.)

Louis was inspired by Dr. Francis Schaeffer, a speaker at Dallas, who described the prevalent spiritual famine. Recognizing the need of his students for this instruction, he convinced the faculty that he needed Schaeffer's *How Shall We Then Live* for his music appreciation course. He began teaching a revolutionary concept of Christian conduct.

As students began repenting, a few of them confided that they had been coerced to engage in homosexual relations with faculty members for grades. He asked them to document their experiences, which he guarded in a safety deposit box. The Lord encouraged us from the first chapter of Jeremiah not to fear those who might harm us. Boldly, Louis prepared a letter exposing this sin and placed copies in all the faculty mailboxes. This added fuel to the fire of resentment, which was already blazing against Louis. Although he was tenured, his contract was not renewed.

During these nine years at LC, the frustration level escalated. Much of it was brought home. Regular contact with Sister by letter, phone, and visits intensified the problems.

In 1973, Louis heard about a Deeper Life Conference to be held in Memphis. The speaker emphasized the home and accepting your mate as a perfect gift from God. My husband returned home, excitedly anticipating next year's conference to be held at Bellvue Baptist Church, also in Memphis. Together, we four participated in the Second Deeper Life Conference. (Special meetings were arranged for the children.) Dr. Adrian Rogers, pastor and coordinator, had brought Dr. Jack Taylor to teach on the home and marriage.

In the midst of the conference, we renewed our vows in a formal Christian wedding ceremony. I dressed in my own wedding gown, Louis in a tuxedo. Omar carried the rings and Sandy carried flowers. Dr. Taylor explained the mystery of Christ and the Church and used us as an example. Then Dr. Rogers reunited us in Christ Jesus. What a blessing it was to be prayed over by those two godly men! At Dr. Taylor's invitation, couples flooded the altar area to renew their vows.

"Now, your home is no longer on sand," taught Dr. Rogers. "It is on the Rock. This doesn't mean it is not going to have problems. It will. It will have storms. It will shake. But it will not fall."

The following three years, Satan contended for our home. Stress at LC, with sedentary teaching in contrast to the physical activity of a music conductor, plus other factors, contributed to a serious health problem for Louis, which adversely affected our personal relations.

The apartment was quiet. The children had long since gone to sleep. Louis and I had retired. He went off to sleep. Restlessly, I rolled out of bed and found my altar in the living room. *Lord, what was the meaning of that ceremony? Was it all a farce? Just for show? This is hell! Our relationship is worse now than ever. Must I stay here? I'll take the children and . . . and . . . but, Lord, where can I go? Take me, Lord, from this misery!* Slipping down from the sofa, I fell on my face before my God. *Lord, here I am, supposedly representing Your Church, Your Bride. And Louis is supposed to be representing You. It's not working! There's a great chasm between us. I can't take this loneliness, suffering, and despair. I won't get up until You answer me. I need Your comfort.*

From the day we stepped off the plane in Florida and were met by Sister, all my dreams had been dashed. Those years under her control had ruined any thought of a successful marriage. I thought back to those dark days of 1969 in my parents' home in Lebanon when it looked like our marriage was over. But then Jesus stepped into my life. In the agony of my spirit, I found the true Lover of my soul.

But now, Lord, Louis stood with me in the presence of four thousand people, in a covenant of marriage, taking me as his wife, vowing to "render to [me] the affection due [me]." And didn't You say that "the husband does not have authority over his own body, but the wife does"? I'm glad he isn't running around with other women. And he's good to the children. But he's no husband to me.

Powers of darkness pressed on me, time after time. No close friend was available to apply a healing balm. At the foot of the cross, I spent hours agonizing in prayer to Him.

I was still raging. I spewed out hurt and bitterness instead of love and mercy. I had to get healed! The Lord walked me backward through my marriage where He pulled up the roots of injuries, fears, and bitterness. It was painful, but the result was glorious!

In spite of the turmoil in our marriage and in my heart, together we responded to an invitation to go to Kentucky to minister at a lay-witness mission sponsored by an individual church. About twenty of us from Jackson were assigned in twos to small groups. A seasoned (middle-aged) prayer warrior was my partner. We were to bring these people to a personal acceptance of Jesus Christ as Savior. Musical Lucy had brought her autoharp and sang about Christ's love for us: "If That Isn't Love?" and "His Eye Is on the Sparrow, and I Know He Watches Me." I told the group how, back in Lebanon, He had revealed Himself to me as the Lover of my soul and had given me eternal life.

In the auditorium, Louis addressed the combined groups: "Do you know for sure that you are saved? This is how we can know: . . ." Several church members, including the pastor's teenage son, confessed their sin, surrendered their lives to Christ, and for the first time found a genuine relationship with Almighty God.

I was seething as God was using my husband in this public ministry. *"Lord, how can you use an inconsistent instrument? I'm really confused. Why do we have to present the best public face, concealing our pain and anger? Putting religious achievement before the sanctity of our marriage? Why can't we be transparent, Lord? When You use Louis, that confirms to him that he is OK and doesn't need any change."*

Unfortunately, Louis felt more responsibility to public ministry than to the position of headship in his home, his role as a husband. A cold, stony wall surrounded his inner feelings. I was shut out. Communication was limited to threats and anger.

Proudly and passionately, I wanted my own way. This wasn't right! *"My child,"* He responded to my heart. *"I walked the Golgotha path which led me to the suffering for which I came to earth. I am leading you in this path to deepen your roots in Me."*

Louis was talking with people at the front of the church; the children were in their special meetings. "Lucy, let's go for a walk." I sensed that she was a woman of prayer, one who knew how to touch God.

"Lucy, I feel like a hypocrite. I told that group of how I met Christ, but I'm not experiencing the abundant life at this moment."

"Hanan, you talked about how back in Lebanon you wanted to be released from Louis, how close you were to divorce. And that agony brought you to Jesus. How is it now?"

"Lucy, people here have confided to me of their marital difficulties and, as a result, some of them have come to Christ. But all I'm doing is hiding pain, trying to save face. To tell you the truth, I feel like this pain is crushing me. Instead of getting better, things have actually gotten worse."

"Hanan, victory comes through fasting and prayer."

"Will you pray with me?"

"Let's set aside Tuesdays. I'll come to your home after your family leaves for school."

Tuesdays I was free. I was no longer studying business at the local college. Tuesdays became the highlight of my life.

"Before we talk to God, we let Him talk to us. God has given us so many wonderful promises to stand on, Hanan."

"Oh, we find a promise and then stand on it?"

"Yes. Here's one: When the enemy shall come in like a flood, the Spirit of the LORD shall lift up a standard against him."*

"What do you make of that, Lucy?"

"Hanan, we wrestle not against flesh and blood, but against principalities, against powers, against the rulers of the darkness of this world, against spiritual wickedness in high places.[†] We need to stand together against the spiritual powers that are fighting against your marital relations."

"Lucy, have I ever told you that witchcraft has been worked against us—against our marriage?"

"No. Tell me about it."

"When Louis went seeking a bride from his old religion in Lebanon in 1964 (he had been in the USA for eleven years and had become a Christian) he met dozens of girls. He fluttered a lot of hearts, two of whom really had their hopes centered on him. Their mothers, too, really wanted him for their daughters. After it was known that he had chosen me, both mothers consulted necromancers who worked magic against our future marriage. There have been other incidents of magic curses put on us."

"Hanan, this calls for prayer with fasting." And so it was agreed. Our Tuesdays became even more special.

Finished with my business course, I still wanted to take some college classes. I saw to it that none were scheduled for Tuesday. Riding to class in my neighbor-friend's car, my spirit was grieved by our small talk. "Let's use these minutes to memorize scripture, Linda."

And so it was that Romans 8 occupied our minds. We kept reviewing the passages studied, all the way through the thirty-eight verses. That chapter bonded us together. "Hanan, I need to learn about this spiritual warfare." And thus it was that our twosome became a threesome.

As we fasted and prayed, I was stripped of pride, self-righteousness, and selfishness. In brokenness, I revealed the pain that I had endured throughout my marriage.

---

* Isaiah 59:19*b*
† Ephesians 6:12

"God makes use of these circumstances, Hanan," comforted Lucy. "He uses them to accomplish His design. When human conduct appears unreasonable, we must look on it as an instrument both of His love and justice."

"Oh, Lucy, when my need is most pressing, my Lord seems to be silent."

"He waits in order to exercise your faith."

"Look at this passage in Luke," added Linda. "'If a son asks for bread from any father among you, will he give him a stone? Or, if he asks for a fish, will he give him a serpent instead of a fish? If you then, being evil, know how to give good gifts to your children, how much more will your Heavenly Father give the Holy Spirit to those who ask Him!'"*

Our marriage was hellish. Louis was in Washington, DC, for a week in a conference. In desperation, I looked for encouragement to divorce him. Rather than confiding in my pastor, I visited a minister of a large church in a nearby city who advised me to see a lawyer. The only one I could think of was a member of our church—the husband of one of my college professors. Although his wife had lovingly befriended me, neither Louis nor I had known him. He eagerly set me up for a divorce, assuring me that I would get a good and quick settlement.

He promised to have the papers ready for my signature within a week. A momentary paralysis held me on the appointed day. The powers of darkness overtook me. The Lord was allowing the enemy to crush me. I knew for sure that the Lover of my soul was chastening me.

My child, I heard God saying. *If you endure chastening God deals with you as with sons; for what son is there whom a father does not chasten? But if you are without chastening, of*

---

* Luke 11:11,13

which all have become partakers, then you are illegitimate
and not [a daughter].*

And my heart replied, *My God, how generously You have
showered me with Your grace. My heart has been unfaithful.
Forgive me, sweet Lover of my soul. Wandering, I have abused
Your grace and offended You. You, instead of rejecting me, still
with open arms covered me with Your fresh love of forgiveness
and mercy, leading me in my life's rugged path. What unfaithfulness on my part, and what faithfulness on Yours. . . . There's
the doorbell!"*

Staggering to the door, I fell into Lucy's comforting arms.
"Lucy, the Lord has stopped me in my tracks. I was para-
lyzed with fear. Satan was attacking me. I can't go through
with this divorce."

"Darling, I praise God that you are listening to *Him.*
How great is His love to us who are His own. It's like an
internal burning fire, purging and purifying our souls as
gold in the furnace of affliction."

"It's easier to cooperate and submit to God," I responded,
"letting Him do His work in me."

"I've seen some who have run away from the pressures,
seeking other means of consolation. Their spiritual growth
was stunted; they stayed babes and were spiritually handi-
capped."

"He's been showing me that it's not enough to escape
hell, but He expects me to become in His image as I allow
Him to work in me."

Rrrrrring.

"Excuse me, I'll get the phone. . . . Yes? Oh, I'm so
sorry. . . . Don't worry about it. Yes, yes. Goodbye."

"What happened?"

---

* Hebrews 12:7

"That's a confirmation from the Lord! The papers are not ready to be signed! The secretary is sick! Praise God!

"Come, dear, let's go feed you!" My precious friend attended to all my needs and left me comforted.

What a surprise when, hours later, Louis returned home a day early! "That last committee meeting was canceled, so we came on home. . . . Hanan, what's the matter?"

"I'm glad you came home early. I've been trying to get your attention, but you didn't listen. Today, I had planned to sign papers of divorce."

"What? What's wrong? There's no reason for a divorce! Let's talk." He looked into my eyes and in a new mood of tenderness drew me to himself.

With a sigh of relief, I looked at him with amazement. *He's taking me seriously! Praise God!*

Mingling our tears, the whole story came out. "Let's go to the lawyer together. Hanan, we'll surprise him! Those proceedings have to be cancelled."

CHAPTER XI

Faith Ministry: 1982

ᘏᗘ

Following the aborted divorce, communication between us opened up. We discussed the possibility of buying our own home. On Tuesday in prayer time, I mentioned it to Lucy, who responded, "I'm going to pray about that!"

"But I don't think he'll really buy one."

"Well, I don't know Louis, but I know my God. What do you want in a house, Hanan?"

"This is silly! Why would God be concerned about what I like in a house?" With her insistence, I finally said, "I like a high ceiling—lots of light, and natural stonework inside." We laughed, and she prayed!

A month later, on my birthday, Louis took me for a ride. "Come," he said as he stopped the car. "I want you to see something." We were looking at a year-old house. Inside I was delighted to see natural stonework, lots of light, and a high ceiling, with three bedrooms and two baths to top it off! The sunny great-room had a cathedral ceiling; sun was streaming in from the dining-room bay windows and shining right into the kitchen. God had answered prayer!

We bought it four years before his teaching position at LC was terminated. When his contract was not renewed, we began thinking, praying, discussing: What next? Along with his doctorate in music, Louis now had his masters of biblical studies from Dallas Theological Seminary. "Hanan, I'm through with teaching music. We're going to serve God by faith."

"What do you mean?" I countered. "We've been living by faith."

"I mean, without the check at the end of the month."

"Oh, that type of faith." In my heart I pondered, *And who's going to pay the mortgage, and take care of us and the children?*

As if he knew what was in my heart, he continued, "God will take care of us when we serve Him. Hudson Taylor learned that if we take care of what's dear to God, He'll take care of what's dear to us. Listen to this, Hanan: in Mark 10: 29 and 30, Jesus answered and said, 'Assuredly, I say to you, there is no one who has left house or brothers or sisters or father or mother or wife or children or lands, for My sake and the gospel's, who shall not receive a hundredfold now in this time—houses and brothers and sisters and mothers and children and lands, with persecutions—and in the age to come, eternal life.'"

Days later, Louis was excited about a phone call. "Remember that man I told you about who has a big church in California? It's a growing church with a varied ministry. I told him I didn't have a job anymore. He was impressed with 1 John 3:17 which says, 'But whoever has this world's goods, and sees his brother in need, and shuts up his heart from him, how does the love of God abide in him?' He has invited me to go out there to work with him."

"If God tells you to go, go," I responded. I reasoned, *God will be my husband. He has always been the great Lover of my soul.*

For seven months Louis taught daily Bible studies. Troubled individuals were brought to him in his office where he counseled with them, leading many to faith in Jesus Christ. Some came troubled by demonic spirits. With the pastor and staff, he participated in casting out evil spirits. Local police brought some of their juvenile criminals from the nearby high school.

Excitedly, Louis called me. "Hanan, you need to come here. God is working miracles. Can you get some time off from your job? The church here will send you a flight ticket."

A friend came to stay with Omar and Sandy and took me to the airport. *Lord, it'll be good to see Louis. Its been months since he left. But You, Lord, have been all I need.* I opened my Bible and read again from Isaiah 54:5:

> For your Maker is your husband,
> The LORD of hosts is His name;
> And your Redeemer is the Holy One. . . .
> He is called the God of the whole earth.

Right after Louis left, You, my Beloved, led me to this job in the department store. And You have used me there to tell others of You, even used it to bring invitations to speak for You in churches! Louis has always been responsible, Lord, and I praise You for that. But the job has eased the pressure.

You have become my refuge and shelter, the faithful lover of my soul! You have taken care of every emergency! Lord,

*remember that trap door of the attic that broke during the storm
and came flying down over me in bed? You steered it away
from me, and then the next day sent a friend to fix it. And when
my car was stalled in the blizzard and I had to abandon it, You
put it on John's heart to call the church to ask if I needed help,
and they sent him to pick it up. He diagnosed the trouble and
fixed it. Thank You, sweet Jesus!*

Approaching the gate I saw my husband's shining countenance. Delighted, I rushed to him.

"Hanan, serving God here has been the most satisfying
time of my life. You're going to love it here. God is going to
use you, Hanan, with the ladies."

The pastor and church family welcomed me warmly.
"We're looking forward to your coming with your children."

"I have an appointment with a school counselor who's
bringing a young rapist to talk with me," said Louis. "Be
praying while I talk with them." Outside the office, I listened through the open door. I was so proud of my husband
as he opened the Bible and showed the youth the conse-
quences of continuing in his way and what would happen if
he repented and chose God's way. He and the counselor both
gave their lives to our Savior as Louis led them in a prayer of
repentance of unbelief. Seeing such mighty works of our Lord
set my heart afire to speed the sale of our house in Tennessee
to join my husband in this exciting ministry.

"That house on the parking lot is vacant," hollered the
pastor from his office. "Would you like to have a look at it,
Hanan."

At that moment our hostess drove up. Pauline's late
husband, a Navy colonel, had attended Louis's Bible studies in a conference the previous year and had come to Christ.
Before his death, he charged Pauline to be attentive to Louis's

needs. In the few days we had been her houseguests, we had become very close. Together we walked to the house. The stench as we opened the door nearly knocked us over. Inside, it was a mess. Pauline looked into my eyes and said, "You are not coming here, Hanan. That's not my Jesus. He gives *good* gifts."

"That doesn't matter. I can clean it and fix it up. Serving Him is more important than houses."

Excitedly, I returned to Jackson to sell our beautiful, clean home and prepare to take the children west. I *wanted* to be with my husband. I *wanted* to be serving the Lord. The children shared my excitement. But buyers were not coming!

Louis came to help me sell the house. No sale! Standing by the sink, I communed with my Lord. *What do you want me to do? . . . Give it away? . . . Lord, You restored my daughter to me after asking us to give her up last year. She was so sick with Rocky Mountain spotted fever. So was her classmate; he died! Louis was no longer teaching at LC; we had no medical insurance. She was misdiagnosed and given wrong medication. We thought we were losing her. But we called the elders who anointed her with oil and prayed over her and You healed her. We've given You ourselves, our children, and now . . . our home?*

"Omar, Sandy!" I rushed into their rooms. "We're going to give our house away!"

We ran to the master bedroom to tell Daddy. We found him on his knees, praying.

"Hanan! The Lord has just been talking to me, too. He was telling me to give up this home. I was asking Him to talk to you and He *has!* Let's call our pastor and tell him."

Before we were able to get in touch with him, we received a letter from California negating the invitation. "Why would they do that, Louis?"

"They say they need to raze the house to provide more parking area. But the real reason is that I taught against the cult of Masonry, and some of the leading elders are part of it."

"Honey," I hugged him. "God is going to reward you for your stand. I'm proud of you. You . . . you've done it again, Louis! You have courageously stood in the lion's den, Daniel! In New York you bucked warnings and stood up for your Lord at your last concert; then you discerned the cultish nature of Dr. Angelica's teaching in that school and church. Here in Jackson, you would not tolerate evil practices but exposed them. And now, again, you were not intimidated by the church elders who are being deceived by false teaching. Honey, I'm proud of you!" The children joined in cheering their daddy on.

A member of an adult Sunday school class that Louis had taught while he was teaching music at the college, was aware of our situation and activities. After praying for us, he invited us to his home for lunch. "Louis and Hanan," he said. "Why don't you start a ministry to reach your own people?"

"How would we start?" Louis asked. "I don't know anything about the paperwork. I'm just interested in teaching the Bible."

"I'll pray that the Lord will start the ministry for you."

That same week, Dr. Walton Padelford was studying for his Sunday school class. God impressed him with 3 John 5–8. *This is what God is calling me to do,* he thought.

"Dr. Hamada," he called on the phone. "Can you come over to my home this afternoon? I need to talk with you."

In his backyard, Dr. Padelford pulled out his Bible. "God spoke to me through this passage in Third John. Listen: 'Beloved, you do faithfully whatever you do for the brethren and for strangers, who have borne witness of your love before the church. If you send them forward on their journey in a manner worthy of God, you will do well, because they went forth for His name's sake, taking nothing from the Gentiles. We therefore ought to receive such, that we may become fellow workers for the truth.'

"Brother, I've been watching how you have stood for the truth. I want to 'send [you] forward on [your] journey in a manner worthy of God. Let me help you start this ministry. I can handle the paperwork."

Louis returned home really excited. "Hanan, can you imagine!? God has given us a man with a Ph.D. in economics to handle our paperwork, our business, our finances! Wow!"

"It doesn't amaze me. This is the character of our God!" I cheered. Within a week, seven friends—pastors, professionals, and businessmen—were installed on our board. Within seven weeks, our ministry was formed; within seven months we were traveling in the United States, Canada, Europe, and the Middle East.

In August of 1982, Louis flew to Europe to participate in a conference for converted Muslims. After preaching on the cost of discipleship, he was called to the office of the director. "Do you mean what you taught tonight, Brother Hamada?"

"Of course," he blurted out. "I meant every word."

"How about going to Israel to evangelize the Druze and the Palestinian Muslims? "

"No, thank you. God hasn't led me to do that."

"Pray about it tonight, Brother Hamada."

Morning came and the director handed Louis a ticket for that afternoon's flight en route to Tel Aviv. Reluctantly, he boarded the plane. While there, God broke his heart because of the mistreatment of the Palestinians. As was his custom, he reached out to those people, listening to them, hearing their concerns, and trying to answer their challenges and questions about the Bible.

Returning to the United States on the plane this discouraged man argued with God: *Lord, I failed You. I thought I knew Your Word. How can I tell these people that You love them when they have heard that the Bible says they are cursed. Lord, I'm confused! Teach me what You are really saying. I came here as a messenger to these people and I haven't helped them at all.*

At home he agonized in prayer and study. He couldn't sleep nights until he saw the error of that teaching and how God's character was vindicated. In many portions of the Bible, he saw the worldwide love of God. From Genesis through the prophets, the life of Christ, and the ministry of the apostles, it became clear to him that God's love is universal. Some Christians had misinterpreted selected passages.

A few weeks later I was on my way to Lebanon to be with my dying father. In him I had seen the highest of human love.

During my stay there, I prevailed upon my father's chauffeur to visit the refugee camps where thousands of people had been recently massacred. The revolting sights, smells, and stories broke my heart. The grief of the bereaved mothers overflowed. Their husbands were gone; their children had been butchered by viciously drugged mercenaries; their hopelessness was irreversible. Physical, mental, and spiritual health were shattered.

Lord, now I can see how Your heart tore asunder for the sin of the world. I cannot comprehend in my human mind the inhumanity of man to man. Those murderers who claim to be "Christians" have never met You. Man without You is baser than the most vicious animal. My heart is bleeding with Yours for these people. They have no hope without You. Lord, vindicate Your name, Your character.

Use us to be Your instrument and healing balm for the survivors of this hellish war. Even to the greatest criminal, Your love abounds. Speak, my God, to my husband to be Your heart to infuse life—eternal life—to these desperately hopeless ones.

On the flight back home, the Holy Spirit affirmed to my heart His unconditional love for these, my people. In our comfortable home in Jackson, we knelt, sobbing, beside our bed and dedicated our life afresh to God on behalf of the Arabs.

CHAPTER XII

1983—1990

T he phone rang and I ran to answer it. "Hanan!"
"Who is speaking? Cousin!" I exclaimed. "Where
are you calling from? How are you and the family?"

"I'm calling from South America," he replied. "We're
fine. How about you?. . . . Hanan, I am very sorry about
Uncle Abraham's death."

"What! Dad is dead?" I screamed.

"You did not know? I'm sorry I called. I thought you
knew."

"No!" I started crying.

"Hanan, he has been dead for weeks! I'm sorry you did
not know, and I had to be the one to give you this bad
news. I'll talk to you again, Cousin. Promise me to be strong
and not to cry. We love you and we will be thinking of you.
Remember your faith in Christ. Goodbye."

Dropping the phone, I rushed to my room, slumped
on my bed, and, burying my face in the covers, cried my
heart out.

I started arguing with God. *Lord, I want to see to believe. Now I understand Your disciple, Doubting Thomas, and relate to him. I trusted You for Daddy's salvation. How about all the verses I claimed with his name and dates written beside them in my Bible? How about all the tears that were shed as I prayed for him? How about the prayers of other saints across this nation and the world? You gave us assurance that Daddy would accept You. What happened? Dear God, I cannot stand the thought of my wonderful father being separated from You. He was so good and so loving. Why couldn't it have been me? My poor mother! Daddy was everything to her. Especially now, with war raging, how is she going to make it without Daddy's love? Now she needs him more than ever and he is gone— through no choice of his own!*

I was talking so fast that I could not hear God talk back to me.

After a night of agonizing and sobbing, drained, I pulled myself out of bed—my eyes swollen shut. As I was combing my hair, the Lord kept tugging on my heart to read Genesis 13:16, where God promised Abraham to multiply his spiritual seed. The cross-reference led me to Romans 4:17, 18, 20-25, 5:1-5:

([A]s it is written, "I have made you a father of many nations") in the presence of Him whom he believed, even God, who gives life to the dead and calls those things which do not exist as though they did; who, contrary to hope, in hope believed, so that he became the father of many nations, according to what was spoken, "So shall your descendants be."

He did not waver at the promise of God through unbelief, but was strengthened in faith, giving glory to God, and being convinced that what he had promised

He was also able to perform. And therefore "it was accounted to him for righteousness."

Now, it was not written for his sake alone that it was imputed to him, but also for us. It shall be imputed to us who believe in Him who raised up Jesus our Lord from the dead, who was delivered up because of our offenses, and was raised because of our justification.

Therefore, having been justified by faith, we have peace with God through our Lord Jesus Christ, through whom also we have access by faith into this grace in which we stand, and rejoice in hope of the glory of God.

And not only that, but we also glory in tribulations, knowing that tribulation produces perseverance; and perseverance, character; and character, hope. Now hope does not disappoint, because the love of God has been poured out in our hearts by the Holy Spirit who was given to us.

After reading those promises, I sat down on my couch. Pondering on these scriptures, the thought of writing a book came to my mind. *I? Write a book ? I cannot!* God said to my heart, *I know you cannot, but I can.*

With paper and pen, I sat down to write. The words started coming like waves, the thoughts like a flood. Not mere impressions, but beautiful and heavenly words to all my people. He took that seed of Dad's death to move me deeply for writing; through the seed of his death, life will come to multitudes. I opened my Bible and read, "Unless a grain of wheat falls into the ground and dies, it remains alone; but if it dies, it produces much grain" (John 12:24).

By faith and through obedience to the Word, I offered to God a sacrifice of praise in the midst of my deep sorrow.

Silence within and without followed . . . a holy hush . . . a great peace.

Agony engulfed me during those months following the death of my father. Where could I turn? I threw myself at God's mercy. My thirsty soul found drink from the wells of my Beloved and nourishment from the Source of my being. Contentment in the midst of anguish and sorrow guarded my spirit. Joy unspeakable filled my soul. I praised Him in my silence and drew strength from His strength.

Lostness, emptiness, and despair accompany the loss of one so dear. Then did I fully appreciate the depth, the breadth, the height, and the totality of God's great love and grace as well as that of my family and Christian friends! Death is the final enemy to be overcome. How bitter, grievous, and hopeless is this life without the Lord our God! He alone sweetens one's life, making it blissful, joyful, hopeful.

"Mommy," comforted Sandy. "You are not alone. We love you."

"What is love?" I asked.

"It's an emotion," piped in Omar.

"Yes, Omar. As humans, we cannot love or know love."

"Love satisfies our human needs," he responded.

"We love the other sex because of a need to be loved and appreciated," I continued. "This is a human instinct, not love. We love parents because we know we are of the same blood and need their security. We love siblings because they are *like* flesh. We love our children because they are a part of us. Human love at best is a selfish love, seeking and surviving on temporary satisfactions. Without God, we know not love, nor how to love!

"Can you quote 1 John 4:16 with me?"

God is love
and he who abides in love
abides in God
and God in him.

Who shall separate us from the love of Christ? Shall tribulation, or distress, or persecution, or famine, or nakedness, or peril, or sword? As it is written: "For Your sake we are killed all day long; We are accounted as sheep for the slaughter." Yet in all these things we are more than conquerors through Him who loved us. For I am persuaded that neither death nor life, nor angels nor principalities nor powers, nor things present nor things to come, nor height nor depth, nor any other created thing, shall be able to separate us from the love of God which is in Christ Jesus our Lord. (Rom. 8:35–39)

133

CHAPTER XIII

Healing of My Marriage
&

PSALM 37

Do not fret because of evildoers,
Nor be envious of the workers of iniquity.
For they shall soon be cut down like the grass,
And wither as the green herb.

Trust in the LORD, and do good;
Dwell in the land, and feed on His faithfulness.
Delight yourself also in the LORD,
And He shall give you the desires of your heart.

Commit your way to the LORD,
Trust also in Him, And He shall bring it to pass.
He shall bring forth your righteousness as the light,
And your justice as the noonday.

Rest in the LORD, and wait patiently for Him;
Do not fret because of him who prospers in his way,
Because of the man who brings wicked schemes to pass.

Cease from anger, and forsake wrath;
Do not fret—it only causes harm.

For evildoers shall be cut off;
But those who wait on the LORD,
They shall inherit the earth.
For yet a little while and the wicked shall be no more;
Indeed, you will look diligently for his place,
But it shall be no more.
But the meek shall inherit the earth,
And shall delight themselves in the abundance of peace.

The wicked plots against the just, and gnashes at him
   with his teeth.
The Lord laughs at him,
For He sees that his day is coming.
The wicked have drawn the sword and have bent their
   bow,
To cast down the poor and needy,
To slay those who are of upright conduct.
Their sword shall enter their own heart,
And their bows shall be broken.

PROVERBS 20:22

Do not say, "I will recompense evil";
Wait for the LORD, and He will save you.

Mother thrilled me with her visit from Lebanon in July
1990. Omar was in Memphis in medical school. I missed
him, but was glad to have his room for Mother.

Then Sister announced her visit. So Mother left to visit
my brother. Receiving Sister at the door, I was amazed by

the divine peace within me. *This isn't me! I could never muster such peace and forgiveness. My Savior, You are showering me with Your grace for an eternal purpose.*

"Welcome to our home, Sister," I said, yielding myself to be directed by His great providence.

Lord, I prayed, *I don't want to be murmuring or complaining. I choose to do Your will.* And the Lover of my soul replied, *I want you to be an instrument of My love, a reflection of My person.*

At this stage in my life, He had already strongly imprinted on my soul that "God is love, and he who abides in love abides in God, and God in him" (1 John 4:16). *Hanan,* I sensed Him saying. *Turn the other cheek. Be My love, My forgiveness to this woman.*

Total dependency on Jesus was my only answer. He brought to my attention Colossians 3:3, "For you died, and your life is hidden with Christ in God," and Galatians 2:20, "It is no longer I who live, but Christ lives in me." *I will enable you,* He assured me, *to forgive, love, serve, and minister to her needs, through My grace.*

His word became life in me. I had ample opportunity to put into practice the Proverb:

> If your enemy is hungry, give him bread to eat;
> And if he is thirsty, give him water to drink;
> For so you will heap coals of fire on his head,
> And the LORD will reward you. (Prov. 25:21-22)

During the three weeks that she stayed, repressed memories rose to the surface. Seven years before, we had been in Italy, ministering life to others. The phone rang in our temporarily rented home. "I'm coming to Milano tomorrow.

Pick me up at the airport." No explanation was given. We welcomed her, shared a hot meal, and warmly visited. Two days later she attacked me physically, emotionally, and spiritually. She cursed me, insulted me, and ordered my departure. "Go to your family! Leave my brother!" she demanded.

Louis watched speechlessly. Never had I experienced such a strong demonic attack—nor have I since. It scared me. I left, running, with only a quickly assembled suitcase and a ticket. A friend put me on the train to Switzerland, where my family and children were vacationing. I cried my heart out on the train. I had neither money nor any European phone number. I was almost lost trying to change trains in a Swiss village. I didn't know the language. But the Lover of my soul sent an angel who directed me to the right train which my brothers met.

I thought I'd never recover from that great trial. Could I ever forgive them for the anguish and emotional pain? My Lord gave me Psalm 37 and Proverbs 20:22.

Now, seven years later, God gave me ample opportunity to "heap coals of fire on her head" by treating her as an honored guest. God only knows what was going on in her heart, but I saw tears in her eyes more than once when she would say, "Hanan, you are a good woman."

"No, Sister. It is Christ, who is in me, who is good."

Cleaning up the dishes after one of her customary acts of hatred, I began discussing the problems of her family. "Sister," I began, "we know that some wicked people plotted against both of your parents, causing their deaths. God said in Psalm 34:16, 'The eyes of the LORD are on the righteous, and His ears are open to their cry. The face of the Lord is against those who do evil, to cut off the remembrance of them from the earth.' You know. . . ."

"I know. I know," she stopped me. "It's like a boomerang. Whatever you wish for others it will come back to you," she continued.

She left without my knowing of her illness. The cancer of the mouth and throat, which had begun seven years before, now spread to her liver. She was given only a short time to live.

Having exhausted the resources of medical science, she was ready to grasp anything. She heard about meetings where people were prayed for and healed. She somehow contacted Addie, a member of David Wilkerson's Times Square Church, who took her to such meetings. In spite of basic differences, Sister found an affinity with this joyous, outspoken, energetic fireball. While Louis and I were overseas on one of our mission trips, her cancer progressed dangerously. Addie visited her faithfully. For the first time in her life, Sister found a friend and opened up to her. She told of the sorrows of her childhood, of her struggles to overcome her gender, of her turmoil and loneliness.

"Addie," she groaned, "I want what my brother's home has. I want that peace." Under Addie's guidance, Sister prayed to Jesus Christ. She trusted in Him. She yielded her life to Him.

Having returned from our overseas mission, we heard that Sister was hospitalized. Louis and Omar flew to New York. She acknowledged their presence but was unable to communicate. It was Addie who filled them in on her final months. From her, they heard of Sister's acceptance of Jesus Christ. After three days in the hospital, she died.

Louis and I had to clean her abode. She had saved all of Louis's letters. How surprised we were to see all that he had written about Jesus Christ and the way of salvation underlined in red! He had repeatedly warned her of her need for Christ—that if she did not believe in Christ, she would be eternally lost.

She had documented her thoughts and activities. I recoiled from seeing the demonic words. God had granted me His Spirit of forgiveness and love. But now, I was shocked to see in writing the great influence she had on my husband, right up to her death. Again, my life was shattered. The emotional pain was crushing. Despair encroached upon me. But, as before, "The Lover of My Soul" protected my spirit and gave me the grace to embrace by faith the hope that is within me, learning "that He who [had] begun a good work in [me would] complete it until the day of Jesus Christ" (Phil. 1:6).

I cried out to Him. Silence. His silence, however, was not a sign of His disapproval, but rather a lesson to exercise my faith to a finer quality through that drastic process of training in order to learn to trust Him regardless of the circumstances. Contrary to my reasoning, God was working in me His eternal purpose for the highest service: to comfort those with the same comfort that He has comforted me.

I cried out that my husband might see the damage of uniting with the devil, against his own flesh—for God has made us one flesh in Him. I knew my Lord would answer, not according to my wishes but according to His will—that which is best for my soul. Even when my heart was dry and barren, the Lord was hearing me. My prayers were not in vain.

Addie was the answer to my prayers! In her Mercedes Benz, her "Jesus car," she took us to one of the meetings to which she had taken Sister. More than listening to the speaker, I was listening to God. At the close of the meeting, people were encouraged to go forward for prayer. With a full heart, I responded. Some of the leaders gathered around me to pray. Their prayers released the pressure that had been building within me. Sobbing, I rushed to the ladies' room. It was Addie who followed me.

"What is it, Dear? What's the matter?"

The burden of my heart poured out.

"Even though I'm a Christian, I'm still human." I told her my agony and concern for my marriage.

After a good cry in her comforting arms, we went out to the car. Addie drove us to the house and stopped the car. "I love you both. I'm concerned about your marriage. I'm not going to let Satan take the victory in this thing! Let's pray that we'll come to grips with this problem."

Repression, feelings, memories, desires, and ideas that are too painful to handle were stuffed down deep within me—some I was not even aware of. It laid like a time bomb ready to explode, which it did.

I cried out to my husband, asking him how he could betray me in that manner. He had no explanation. I then realized for the first time in my life the power of darkness and what we are truly fighting against: not flesh and blood, but principalities and powers in dark places (Eph. 6:12, 2 Cor. 10:4–5). Then I truly comprehended the measure of that powerful force. The apartment seemed to be haunted, too.

On our knees, we fell and, with sobbing and tears, renounced these demonic generations, submitted to God's Spirit, repented and asked for forgiveness. The Holy Spirit opened the gates of our souls. Like springs, love and emotion that had nearly dried up for years, burst through the desert of our spirit with healing and balsam of ointment to replace bitterness with forgiveness and love.

During that climactic trial, I discovered that all my happiness—spiritual, temporal, and eternal was conceivable only by submitting myself to Him, by allowing Him to do in me and with me as He pleases. By total dependency on His Spirit, He was making me now in the image of His Son that I might be one with my Beloved.

In my spirit, I communed with my God: *How bitter, grievous, and hopeless this life can be without You, O God. You make it sweet, joyful, and hopeful to me. It makes no difference about my interest and reputation. My desire is You, Lord. I want to behold Your beauty.*

I was learning that even spirit-filled Christians suffer and question and shrink as we follow. Out of weakness, we are made strong. As our Lord cried out, "If it is possible, let this cup pass from Me, nevertheless, not as I will, but as Thou wilt." We are triumphant through Christ to endure our appointed cross.

My soul was kept in contentment even in the midst of anguish and sorrow. In Him I had joy unspeakable. I praised Him in silence and drew from His strength in my weakness.

"Your name, O Lord, is ointment, poured forth. Therefore the virgins love you" (Song of Sol. 1:3). Christ then captivated our hearts as one, and our relationship began to draw strength from God's strength, wisdom from God's wisdom.

Now I understood. Like the kernel of corn, I had to die. The Lord lovingly drew me into Him by internal transformation. He, the Lover of my soul, became the absolute Master of my heart in this everlasting marriage.

For your Maker is your husband, The LORD of hosts is His name;

And your Redeemer is the holy One. . . .;
He is called the God of the whole earth.

For the Lord has called you
Like a woman forsaken and grieved in spirit,
Like a youthful wife when you were refused
Says your God. (Isa. 54:5–6)

The Lord took me through stages and walked me back through places in my marriage where scars of unforgiveness and bitterness had developed. He exposed me to myself in order to perform a spiritual surgery, pulling and cutting those mortal roots. Facing the truth about one's self is a painful process. The end, however, is praiseworthy and glorious.

In the gospel, the Lord commands love and forgiveness. Love is not dependent on the way we feel, but rather it is an act of faith in obedience to His Word.

We Christians have failed in this area—talking love but not walking it. Jesus said, "By this all will know that you are My disciples, if you have love for one another" (John 13:35).

Many have been deceived by covering up to save face; they endure a bad marriage by living in an unloving relationship in disobedience to the Almighty God.

Love is the whole impetus and thrust of the New Testament. In marriage, the Lord allows this commandment to develop. It is two people committed to each other for better or for worse—in love. It is God's design where two adults grow together in His character. It is like a sandpaper to smooth out the rough edges in our character. It is abrasive on one side and smooth on the other, bitter on one side and sweet on the other. It is the testing lab of Christianity and a picture of God's plan for us.

Marriage is the little world where two people experience death, resurrection, and redemption—a reflection of God and His church. It is not only a place where the desires

143

of the flesh are fulfilled or an enjoyable way to procreate and populate the earth. To view it this way is to miss God's purpose and intention. It is the instrument which God uses to straighten up our rebellious wicked hearts and total depravity. It is a commitment—a pledge to work for redemption in each other's lives. Some of us have a harder task than others, but His work in us and His sufficiency and grace carries us through the storms of life and marriage.

Husbands and wives may be basically incompatible. The home is God's classroom for molding and shaping us into mature people. Shares Peter Marshall, from the movie *A Man Called Peter*:

> Marriage is a fusion of two hearts, the union of two lives, the coming together of two tributaries which after being joined in marriage, will flow in the same channel in the same direction. . . .carrying the same burden of responsibility and obligation.

CHAPTER XIV

Together in His Service

B y a series of miracles, through His Spirit and by the strokes of His hammer, the Lord shaped us and prepared us to launch out by faith, in obedience to the call of God. Step by step, He led us and provided the funds, making it possible for us to go at the time He appointed, not taking credit for any strength and talent of our own but knowing full well that we owe it all to Him. "I am the vine, you are the branches. He who abides in Me, and I in him, bears much fruit, for without Me, you can do nothing" (John 15:5).

He called us as His ambassadors to be His Light in a dark and evil world—to be the salt of the earth, wholly at His disposal for this, His eternal purpose.

Both Louis and I, through all our trials, knew by now that God did not create us to live for our own selfish purpose, but to be instruments of His glory through experiences of bitter and sweet. We must be a road map for others to relate to in the different areas they are hurting, to be transparent as we expose our life. He wants us to peel off our pride by sharing with others our hurt and weakness so they might know His sufficiency and faithfulness.

Even before our marriage was healed, God, in His sovereign will designed to use us. Louis's books *God Loves the Arabs Too* and *Understanding the Arab World* opened up doors in the United States, Canada, Europe, and the Middle East. God used us in churches, Bible schools, seminaries, colleges, universities, and missions. We were speaking at conferences, conducting seminars, teaching students, recruiting missionaries, training missionaries, challenging people. We were bringing Arab awareness with emphasis on God's indiscriminate love. We have witnessed changed hearts, broken walls of pride and prejudice, and a new view of the world through the eyes of the Savior. Some have come to salvation.

Summer 1990 was special. My dear beloved mother was my guest. She and I spent many hours deeply talking and reminiscing. She asked me questions one night as we sat up late in our great-room.

"Hanan, I have been questioning my destiny and the why of my being," she sighed. "I have been watching you and wondering why can't I have this peace you have."

"Mom, if you only believe, if your faith is as small as the mustard seed . . . ," I tenderly answered as I looked out into the floodlights illuminating our back yard. "Believe in Him, our Savior," I added.

"How do you know what you believe in, is not just a beautiful illusion? I mean, you truly have changed: Your marriage is much better. I cannot deny that, but maybe it's just a dream."

"Maybe it is," I answered kindly. As I was watching the green branches of the strong oak tree bending before the wind, I prayed silently that the wind of the Spirit would blow across her heart and breathe new life into her. "I can't prove that it's not. I can only tell you that if it is a dream, it is the best dream that mankind has ever had.

"I do not believe it is just a dream. His reality and real person changed all my being and destiny. It is the life without Christ that is the dream, a nightmare. Coming to Jesus Christ is the true awakening."

"Inside of me, I know there is God but I do not know Him personally and intimately like you know Him. Oh, how I yearn for that, Hanan."

Looking at the stars and the moon reflecting their light through our sky-windows, I quoted Psalm 19:1–3 and Romans 1:20:

> The heavens declare the glory of God; and the firmament shows His handiwork. Day unto day utters speech, and night unto night reveals knowledge. There is no speech nor language where their voice is not heard.
>
> For since the creation of the world His invisible attributes are clearly seen, being understood by the things that are made, even His eternal power and Godhead, so that they are without excuse,

She listened deeply as I read His word. Into my eyes she looked. I held her hands tightly. Touched by His love and mine, she said, "Hanan, let us pray that He will come into my life, too."

Five years earlier, two years after Dad's death, the Lord confirmed to me His destiny. My sister-in-law Susan, whom I won to Christ in 1973 from the occult and demon possession, was then living in the United Arab Emirates. She returned to Tennessee to visit with her ailing father. "Hanan," she said. "I think you should know that your family has been wondering about your Dad's last words. As he was dying, he mumbled, 'It is worth what I went through to know what I know now.'

"Hanan, what do you think? Could it be he came to know our Savior before he passed away?"

"Wow!" I screamed. "What a confirmation! I waited two years for my Lord to let me know. Praise His holy name! 'Shall not the Judge of all the earth do right?'" (Gen. 18:25)

CHAPTER XV

Behold My Beloved!

&

Behold my Beloved, my Love, my Bridegroom. He cometh out of His chamber. The Sun of the Morning, breaking through the piercing darkness of my life; with a great and mighty light shining and illuminating my spirit, soul, and being; taking me away from the pain, suffering, scars, and memories; healing me deep in my spirit with His majestic mercy.

Behold my Beloved, my Bridegroom, The Lover of My Soul. He is beautiful, handsome, wonderful, and altogether lovely. The smell of perfume precedes His arrival, breathing on me the breath of life; igniting my heart with fire from above, melting me like wax from within, with His great love.

Behold my Beloved, The Lover of My Soul. His love causes my heart to flutter and race, for I am in love with my Beloved. He is decked with beauty, perfection, and excellence! Behold His loveliness, the fairest of all. My Beloved takes my breath away with awe, wonder, and amazement as I behold Him.

Behold my Beloved, my Love, The Lover of My Soul cometh with great company, ministering angels are before Him, around Him, underneath Him, and above Him. He is leaping over the mountains with His majesty, filling the earth with His authority. Sovereignly overshadowing me and covering me with the majesty of His wings, like a loving parent, drawing me into His bosom with His mighty arms. His love is better than life!

My Beloved, The Lover of My Soul, my Shepherd, I delight in You, under Your shadow I lay. I bask in Your warmth, truth, and guidance. You put before me Your banqueting table, Your banner over me is love!

My Beloved, my Love, Your voice is like many waters, Your countenance is like the mountains of Lebanon. Your mouth is like honey and the honeycomb, Your eyes are piercing. You see through my innermost being. Your love is unconditional. You comfort and protect me. Your words are like a sword and arrows in my spirit. They change me and mold me. Your banner over me is love!

My Beloved calleth me and says, "Come away my virgin, My love, let us spend time together." To the garden we go. There I speak to my Beloved and He speaks to me. As I nourish from His love, He whispers love in my ears and sweetly and patiently He listens to me. He tells me of His deep faithful love and that the present pains, hurts, sufferings, and disappointments will soon vanish away.

My Beloved, my King, my Rock, my Fortress, the Shelter and Refuge of my life, You take me away to Your secret places and as I behold You and Your lovely face, I weep from the depth of my being in appreciation of Your deep, deep love and care. I am Yours and You are mine. Everything becomes insignificant in the shadow of Your love.

My Beloved, my God, You surround me with favor. You are the One that my heart adores and is after. I seek You and yearn for You. You are the only One that satisfies. You are the One that my soul loveth. I hold You tight and do not want You to go. I cling to You as the branch clings to the vine. You are the One I drink and nourish from. You ravish me with fruit, abundant fruit. You dress me up with Your robe of righteousness. You bestow on me much gifts and jewels. My soul loveth You!

My Beloved, even in the night as I go to sleep You are in my heart, my thoughts, my dreams. My heart yearns for You, wanting to know You intimately. I am blessed and happy and full of joy. You are generous, very generous to me, You shower me with Your love. Your banner over me is love!

My Beloved, You are the fairest of ten thousand. Perfect in holiness, excellent in beauty. My heart cries for You. Come my King, my Love, my God, my LORD, The Lover of My Soul. Come quickly! I say come, Your virgins adore You and are anxiously awaiting You. Our Bridegroom, our Love, our Beloved Jesus come!

Behold my Beloved, my King cometh; thousands plus thousands minister to Him. Ten thousands times ten thousands stood before Him. The earth shook and rumbled at His presence. The LORD, the Righteous Judge and the Lawgiver is He. The King of Kings, Almighty God, the great I Am, and Ancient of Days are His names. The Alpha and Omega, the Beginning and the Ending, sitting on His throne. His hair is as white as snow, His eyes like fire and His voice as many waters. His Kingdom and dominion are everlasting forevermore!

Behold my Beloved, my Love cometh! The LORD of Hosts, My Prince, the Prince of Peace is His name. The

Author and Finisher of my faith is He. The Lamb on the throne, my Hiding Place and Saving Grace. With the shout of a trumpet breaking through the heavens He comes forth. This is my Beloved and this is my Love!

Behold my Beloved, my LORD, Holy! Holy! Holy! is He. The whole earth is full of His glory. Who am I, my Beloved, that You bestow Your goodness and mercy on me? With your precious blood atone me and put my sins out of sight, as far as the east from the west. My soul loveth You, my spirit adores You! You truly are The Lover of My Soul! Come please, come my LORD, my God. Hallelujah and hallelujah, my soul knoweth quite well.

CHAPTER XVI

Reflections from My Early Christian Life

❧

WHO AM I?

I am but one of God's special creations, a person. I am so insignificant, one of billions, but yet I am incredibly important to God. Traveling around the world in the skies just a few thousand feet high, I look down to the earth and think, *What is man? Why does God love mankind?* It seems that we are puny, almost invisible down on earth, and yet God loves us and mankind is important to Him (Ps. 139, Jer. 1, Isa. 49:1,5).

WHAT IS LIFE ALL ABOUT?

As a child, I had dreams to be everything and the best. *What is the best? What is everything?* He, the Creator, the same God that made everything, also knit me together in my mother's womb exactly with the right material. He wanted me to have and to look exactly like I do. Amazed, I ask:

Why was I born into that wonderful family?
Why was I born a wanted child?
Why was I loved and cared for?
Why was I born in Lebanon?
Why? Why? And why? It will never end!

Myriad questions run through my mind. Acceptance and submission are the key. Our minds do not have the answer and never will. See Isaiah 26:3, Jeremiah 29:11; 2 Chronicles 16:9.

Acceptance to how we are made,
Surrender to Him who made us,
Submission to situations we cannot change,
This is, trusting faith in Him who loves us.
This gives peace and contentment

ARE WE IN CONTROL OF OUR LIVES?

No, is the answer! Everything I dreamed, I never reached. Everything I wanted, I did not get. For years, war raged within me until I submitted to the God that made me. Before He took control of me, race as I might, I could never reach my goal. When I submitted to Him, I learned contentment. It was not easy: The flesh continued to seek its own reward but the new spiritual nature demanded righteous choices.

What shall we say then? Shall we continue in sin that
grace may abound? Certainly not! How shall we who died
to sin live any longer in it? . . . For to be carnally minded
is death, but to be spiritually minded is life and peace.
(Rom. 6:1–2; 8:6)

I have learned to sit, to think, to pray and meditate. I am
not afraid of my life's reality. "Whereas you do not know
what will happen tomorrow. For what is your life? It is
even a vapor, that appears for a little time, and then van-
ishes away." (James. 4:14)

He is the only real and immutable thing in my life, and
I know that my life and all that happens in it will pass, but
He will remain. He has always been; He is always there; He
will always be. Even though I cannot fully understand that,
I believe it. The belief started as a selfish need for security,
but now it is deeper than that; now it is the source of my
life. He exists. He made me. Therefore I am.

THE SIN OF EVE

God supplied all her needs. God had provided all to
fulfill her spiritual desires within her grasp. The desires of
the flesh fascinated her and she wanted to partake of it also.
She beheld the fruit. Its fragrance tantalized her. She
touched—and then consumed the sin. In choosing to satisfy the physical desire, she relinquished the gift of life; not
only for herself, but also for her husband (Gen. 3).

Epilogue

⁂

L ouis Bahjat, I am convinced that it was the Lord that brought you to me, that I might come through these difficult circumstances to the knowledge of Him. Thank you for being a good provider for me and the children. Thank you for being focused on the call that God created you to do. I appreciate you being unmovable to defend His word, not fearing people's faces (Jer. 1:17).

Omar, my son, you are truly a treasure that every parent dreams to have. You have touched my life deeply by your charismatic and pure Christlike character; a man of integrity and high morals. You excelled and achieved in spite of difficult circumstances. Thank you for your love that never fails. I pray that God will grant you the fullness of His knowledge and for your heart to be rooted deeply in His love of eternal values (Matt. 6:19–21).

Sandy, my precious daughter, you are truly an answer of prayer. You have influenced my life with your depth and godly wisdom. Thank you for having a strong character and loyalty. You have blossomed to be a Proverbs 31 woman;

your worth is truly above treasures. For this reason I bow my knees to the LORD that He might reveal to you the riches of His glory and the depth of His love, to be strengthened by His spirit in your inner soul (Eph. 3:14–21).

I thank God for you both always, for all the joy and richness you have brought to my life. You truly are a reward and a gift from the LORD. Thank you, Omar, for bringing Tara to also be my daughter; and you, Sandy, for bringing Andrew to be another son. Thank you, both of you, for giving us Nathan, our first grandchild, and a treasure for God.

Elizabeth Taylor, my dear sister and friend, thank you for being an exemplary of a godly woman, a lover of God, truly His wise virgin (Matt. 25:4). You have shaped my life deeply for eternity! "Watch, stand fast in the faith, be brave, be strong. Let all that you do be done with love" is what I have learned from you (1 Cor. 16:13–14). Thank you, Elizabeth, for the many hours you took me with you to the holy of holies, on our knees in His presence to worship and adore Him. Thank you for teaching me to enjoy my Beloved in the depth of His glory. I will cherish those moments forever and ever!

Thank you, Sherry Caldwell, for your deep knowledge and wisdom of Him and His word. Thank you that our friendship has not been shallow and vain, but He has always been the center and focus of our conversation, being the silent Listener. He always drew near (Luke 24:15, 30, 32). The depth of His treasures will always go with me wherever I go!

Thank you, sweet Denny Wilkes, my loyal friend, "A friend loves at all times and a brother (sister) is born for adversity" (Prov. 17:17). Thank you for all the times you spent on your knees agonizing with me in prayer for my father and mother's souls, for your deep unconditional love to my mother. You reaped what you sowed! I am forever grateful for your unselfish kindred spirit. My life is not the same because of you!

Thank you, J. K. and Becky Baker, for all these years of standing with us through the ups and downs, the bitter and sweet. You have been a reflection of His character, a fragrance of His knowledge, an epistle written on our hearts, known and read by all men. We will always thank God for you (2 Cor. 3:2)!

Thank you, Becky Arendale, for being my American mother since I was twenty-five. Thank you for all the prayers we prayed together that we lived to see fulfilled. I am forever grateful! (Prov. 27:9).

Thank you, Opal Johnson, for your unconditional love. ". . .but there is a friend that sticks closer than a brother [or sister]" (Prov. 18:24b).

I could go on and on for all of you, my family and friends, who truly have influenced and touched my life for eternity. But you know who you are here and there and all over the world. Thank you for your prayers, love, giving, and standing with us as we labor together for Him and His glory (1 Cor. 3:9).

Louis and me—1967

Louis and me—1998

Omar (left) is now a physician, an assistant professor, and director of predoctoral affairs at the University of Tennessee Department of Family Medicine. He is also a flight surgeon with the Special
Forces. Omar is married to Tara, who is also a physician in Internal Medicine and Pediatrics.

Sandy holds her master's degree in clinical psychology from
Wheaton Graduate School. She is married to Andrew Combs, a
chiropractor.

Hanan Hamada may be contacted
for speaking engagements and
to order additional copies of

send $10.99 plus $3.95 shipping and handling to:

Mrs. Hanan Hamada
P.O. Box 3333
Jackson, TN 38303

Fax (901) 668-7102
lhamada@iname.com